Questions of You
and the Struggle
of Collaborative Life

Studies in the
Postmodern Theory of Education

Joe L. Kincheloe and Shirley R. Steinberg
General Editors

Vol. 104

PETER LANG
New York • Washington, D.C./Baltimore • Boston • Bern
Frankfurt am Main • Berlin • Brussels • Vienna • Canterbury

Nicholas Paley and Janice Jipson

Questions of You and the Struggle of Collaborative Life

PETER LANG
New York • Washington, D.C./Baltimore • Boston • Bern
Frankfurt am Main • Berlin • Brussels • Vienna • Canterbury

Library of Congress Cataloging-in-Publication Data

Paley, Nicholas.
Questions of you and the struggle of collaborative life /
Nicholas Paley and Janice Jipson.
p. cm. — (Counterpoints; vol. 104)
Includes bibliographical references (p.).
1. Education—Research—Methodology. I. Jipson, Janice. II. Title. III. Series.
IV. Series: Counterpoints (New York, N.Y.); vol. 104.
LB1028.J57   370'.7'2—dc21   98-30630
ISBN 0-8204-4251-5
ISSN 1058-1634

Die Deutsche Bibliothek-CIP-Einheitsaufnahme

Paley, Nicholas:
Questions of you and the struggle of collaborative life /
Nicholas Paley and Janice Jipson.
—New York; Washington, D.C./Baltimore; Boston; Bern;
Frankfurt am Main; Berlin; Brussels; Vienna; Canterbury: Lang.
(Counterpoints; Vol. 104)
ISBN 0-8204-4251-8

Cover design by Lisa Dillon
Cover art appears courtesy of Galerie Darthea Speyer, Paris
"Au Fond" by Ed Paschke 1991
oil on linen, 78" x 84"
Collection MACM (Musée d'art contemporain, Marseille)

The paper in this book meets the guidelines for permanence and durability
of the Committee on Production Guidelines for Book Longevity
of the Council of Library Resources.

© 2000 Peter Lang Publishing, Inc., New York

Printed in the United States of America

Dedication

To Jen, Emily, & Erik, who teach me daily about questions,
possibility, delight;
and for Lin— still thousands of miles to go . . .

Contents

Contents

Acknowledgments

Writing collaboratively is a consuming process and requires the support and understanding of families, friends, and coworkers. We would like to acknowledge the many individuals who have contributed to the creation of this book. Our appreciation, first of all, to Joe Kincheloe and Shirley Steinberg, our companions in this journey of research exploration. Our thanks also to our colleagues at National Louis University and George Washington University who have provided us with collegial support throughout the process of developing this work. Adding vitality to our project were the many students who have been a source of feedback and inspiration for us. Thanks also to Chris Myers and his staff at Peter Lang Publishing for providing the editorial and technical support that enabled us to actually produce the book.

We would also like to acknowledge the cooperation of the following publications for permission to reprint materials which originally appeared in their journals. Chapter 2 originally appeared in briefer form in *English Education 29* (1), 59–69. A version of Chapter 3 was initially presented at the annual meeting of the American Educational Research Association, San

Francisco, California, April, 1989 and was later published in *English Education* 23 (3), 14–159. Chapter 5 originally appeared in *Educational Foundations* 6 (2), 21–33. Chapter 8 appeared in *Taboo: The Journal of Culture and Education* 2 (2), 269; the infrared satellite photograph of Hurricane Andrew is courtesy of the National Oceanic and Atmospheric Administration, Silver Spring, Maryland. Sections of Chapter 7 are forthcoming in different form in *Theory Into Practice*, special issue on New Visions of Mentoring Research; and in *The International Journal of Leadership in Education*, published by Taylor & Francis Ltd.

Finally, we would like to thank Galerie Darthea Speyer, the Museum of Contemporary Art, Marseille, and Ed Paschke for permission to reproduce the artwork which appears on the book cover.

Many of you have chosen, as we have, to do collaborative work. For some of you, collaboration may extend from your shared interest in particular theoretical, methodological, or political questions. For others of you, the imperative to work together may be strategic. Perhaps, like us, you engage in collaborative work because of your recognition that what you can create together is more satisfying, richer than what you could accomplish alone. For others, collaboration may develop for reasons that are deeply personal. Working together can provide an alternative to the isolation and loneliness of the individual research and writing experience, and can affirm the joyousness of learning within a social context.

When we began to work together nearly three decades ago as teaching colleagues, our motivations along these lines were not very exact or well-articulated. Working together in a shared academic environment, we found that our "collaboration" evolved out of an initial physical proximity, but also from similar personal needs as we each struggled to navigate the rough waters of the difficult beginnings of an academic career. At that time our collaborative work was a process that seemed to emerge day by day, even when we were unaware that collaboration was what we were doing.

Now, nearly three decades later, we are able to name as "collaborative" our work together, but we find ourselves still struggling with basic questions of what collaboration really means and how it does and does not take place. We wonder about its relation to our individual and social worlds, and its value in helping us understand ourselves and our present environments. We puzzle, still, over how to articulate these concerns and represent the issues they have raised.

Sensing that many of you who also work collaboratively may share some of our questions, we offer these reflections on our experiences as collaborative researchers. We hope that our work may be useful to you in clarifying— or complicating— your own collaborative efforts.

We don't see things as they are;
we see them as we are.
— Anaïs Nin

Chapter One

Making Collaborative Life

What is the nature of collaboration? How do collaborative efforts function within the research process? What connections do individuals develop with each other while working in similar analytic space? How do these associations contribute to the experience of thinking and writing, knowing and being? How can the processes of collaboration be researched, and how can they be represented? What kinds of questions about analytic practice are generated by collaborative inquiry as part of the process of doing educational research?

This is a book that explores the nature of the collaborative experience within the location of personal reference. Its focus is on our own twenty-five-year history as colleagues, teachers, researchers, and close friends; and the book experiments with this experience in order to examine the complex factors involved as two people work together to understand the conceptual perspectives they develop, the interpretive positions they create, and the multiple, shifting possibilities for personal and social change at stake in such searching and making. Central to this inquiry is the belief that the study of such activity is expressive of important educational and relational issues, and their intersections with intersubjectivity, self-representation, and personal imagination. It is our hope that such situated analysis may provide new understandings about the interaction of these forces, and the often conflicting conditions of a collaborative pedagogy and research practice. As such, it attempts to explore what we may know, how we might know, and in what kinds of ways we may express both our questions and understandings of the collaborative experience.

* * *

As with most books, there is a history behind this writing project. For the past several years we have been struggling as educational researchers to find an appropriate way to study the nature of doing collaborative work. At first, we considered presenting a series of our research studies with critical commentary, an approach that we subsequently modified and redeveloped, but ultimately found unsatisfactory in capturing the complexities of our actual collaborative experience. We began to realize that what we wished to consider was not the sum of the research productions completed during our collaborations, but the on-going stories of the collaborative process as they provide occasions to search for, remember, and examine the many kinds of relations that constitute that experience. For us, these processes and dynamics came to include the following practices: developing an intellectual life; negotiating the phenomena of power, knowledge, language, and identity; and creating contexts for dialogue to occur across these diverse discursive and emotional productions. Given these realizations, we systematically began to explore the twisting and often-retraced paths of our collaborations across nearly three decades of academic life, documenting, in the analytic tradition of teacher reflexivity, their congruences and quarrelings "from front to back and from back to front; from top to bottom, from bottom to top, from side to side and corner to corner" (Ashton-Warner, 1963, pp. 19–20). By examining the processes of our work together in this way and our relations to our work and to each other, we sought to better understand how collaboration does and does not take place, and how it, like learning, can function as a living space "where people can still be changed" (Ashton-Warner, 1963, p. 12).

Our simultaneous work on alternative forms of research production helped us further develop our project. A major part of this approach involved experimenting with the methodologies of "multiple voice and response" (Paley, 1995, p. 185), and text/intertext (Jipson & Paley, 1997). These strategies helped us better problematize and display the complex forces at issue in the give-take, push-pull energies of our working relationship. They also freed us to juxtapose phenomena, events, and understandings within a kind of bricolage in order to restore the often contradictory, non-sequential dynamics of lived experience and memory. By integrating diversified perspectives, structures, and alternative representational devices to analyze our shared experience, we felt it was more possible to express the complicated texture of our collaborations both as (inter-)personal process and as metaphor for doing educational work. It was from this continuing, often recursive struggle to examine the dynamics of our collaborative experience and from the always changing conditions of our work together that the writing for this book eventually emerged.

* * *

Questions of You and the Struggle of Collaborative Life provides a multi-layered scan of our shared work. In this exploration, we have identified six seemingly discrete but often overlapping layers that appear to characterize the structure of our collaborative process. The layers are woven through each chapter in different ways and into different motifs and designs. In some chapters, certain layers appear to be more sustained than in others, becoming broader or narrower as they re-present the development of our thinking. This layered construction enables us to re-create our overall experience of collaboration in its multiple forms; and, in the process of creating each new chapter, new understandings are over-layered onto existing ones, so that the accumulation grows in density and texture, and meanings become both a more timely and a more archaic version of what they once were. While the exact focus and dimensions of each chapter vary, and although the ways that "content" is presented is generally asynchronous from chapter to chapter, we recognize the usefulness of these multiple layerings, since such constructions create spaces for the discrepancies, patternings, motifs, and major and minor colorings of experience to emerge. This layered structure helps us read collaboration as familiar and strange, actual and metaphoric, possible and problematic, for the more we recognize ourselves in such contested and sometimes contradictory experience, "the more it will be possible for [us] . . . to be creative agents[s] of history at the same time [we are] reinvented by history" (Freire, 1998, p. 52).

Collaboration Always Has a Story

One layer in this process is the actual collaboration we have shared as students, teachers, researchers, and friends. This layer seems to take the form of a literal and chronological narrative, as we describe and inscribe events, occurrences, and phenomena that develop within and across our academic and personal lives. In this layer, it seems as if we're writing "on the line," or telling a story, as we present "real events" that we struggled within our thinking and work together. So we write from our direct experience about how the self connects with another in actual, academic space; we name the ways that roles, agendas, and identities are formed and re-formed in the collaborative process; and we testify, through our collective memory, to the details and social occurrences of our work together in the real world. In this layer, we build out from the actual to create a chronology of experience which then suggests specific patterns, contours, and interconnections among ideas, facts, and intentions. Presenting our work this way creates opportunities "to articulate the themes of [our] existence and to reflect on those themes until [we] know [ourselves] to be in the world, naming what has been up to then obscure" (Greene, 1978, p. 19). But there are always many sides to chronology, and the stories we write also help us understand our often conflicting perceptions of it. More than just an accumulation of facts then, these stories create multiple points for posing questions about "the factual" and for provoking dialogue about the choices we made that we could not have expected when we began. So even as we make concrete efforts to document our experiences through details of real events and structured, temporal order, new collaborative interpretations are already leaking through these documentations, complicating notions of cohesiveness, extending the memories of these original experiences, and creating a second, related layer of interpretation.

Collaboration and Its Double

This layer is formed by our conscious exploration of the interpersonal dynamics and patterns apparent across the history of our experience together. Sometimes it seems that this layer (of collaboration) takes the form of shared analytic activity. As we negotiate the chronology of our collaborative work, we find ourselves inevitably engaged in a re-vision and transformation of the original experience through the process of our analysis, focusing on questions of who we might really have been, what might actually have happened, and what it possibly meant. In this layer, it appears as if we're writing "against the line," disturbing the actual and its historical flows in order to transform the actual— making room for conjectures and analytic readings about our collaborative efforts that may have been obscured by the linear. Often the writing in this layer seems to interrupt the chronology we make, questioning our organization of ideas, facts, and intentions into forms of destiny, or narratives of progress, or story. It is through this simultaneous deconstruction and reconstruction of the linear and of the ways our collaborations have developed over the years that we can differently analyze patterns of commitment, of process. In many ways, this exploration often takes the form of recursive and reiterated dialogue, of "non-narrative narrativity" (Britzman, 1994), and is always self-referenced yet open to reorganization and renewal.

Collaboration Across Representational Borders

Yet another layer of our collaborative project involves producing this book and representing our work in ways that reflect the complexity of collaborative life. This layer is produced through a diversified methodological approach that is organized around a number of changing and sometimes discordant heuristic perspectives representing narrative, autobiographic, interrogative, fictive, poetic, documentary, and theoretic genres. In the telling and retelling of our experience from these varying perspectives, we struggle with "the mysterious work of remembrance" (Benjamin, cited in Lather, 1999, p. 3), and with the difficulties of writing the unmediated real— seeking to restore in present time the meaning— rather than merely the letter— of the shifting, simultaneous, and always changing versions of our experience, the intensity and vacillation of our feelings toward each other and to the work itself, and the ever-multiplying understandings of our selves and our work together. As we consciously engage in this task of reflection and re-creation, constructing new material from the material of our own original making and memory, we frequently work against the grain of functional analysis and representation, venturing other methodologies and displays for straight-line thinking. Such processes help us "activate the wider possibilities of human intelligence" (Eisner, 1997, p. 8) as we struggle to create a medium for understanding how collaboration functions across multiple realms, thus freeing ourselves to better "see" what it may be.

Collaboration Is Both Mirror and Lens

Another layer within the collaborative process is formed through our reflective analysis of the project as a whole. Sometimes this layer appears through our conscious discussion of how (and why) we have chosen to represent our experiences across the history of our work together, and how our multiple understandings of the experiences themselves emerged. Here, we collaborate again, as we focus on the conditions/demands of language and meaning, connotation and interpretation, reality and sur-reality as they insert themselves in the reconstruction and re-presentation of the whole of our collaborative life together, and apart. These issues form an analytic mirror that reflects our assumptions, our preferred modes of discourse, and our chosen practices in the research world. These issues also serve as a lens through which we can refocus on our struggles with power, knowledge, language, and identity relations. Yet even as we work to clarify these phenomena to ourselves and to each other, we find ourselves identifying still other forces, other insights into the collaborative process, and we realize that we are always beginning anew. So each time we think our understanding of our experience is finally clear, another perspective always seems to present itself. Sometimes these meta-reflections take the form of writing that dances across the page, uncertain of its direction as it verges into even more complicated conditions/demands of dialogue, voice, trust, interest, and love.

Collaboration Is a Complex Weave

Like Bateson (1990), we too recognize collaboration as being a "complex weave" (p. 10) formed from "layers of involvement" (p. 82). This weave and these layers are, as much as anything, constituted through the threadings of our everyday lives and work together: telephone conversations long into the night; shared teaching experiences; this moment around an old oak table where we sit and write these words in the April sunlight; the pain of too many broken promises; a box of insights one of us keeps searching for in our dreams; our commitment to shared voice; fractures in commitment; months of long silence masquerading as work. Each of these involvements contributes to the hopes and trade-offs we make as we open our mouths to speak. So there is really no one pattern we make from all this but many: trellised, fervent, complementary, difficult, isolated, conflicting, interdependent, free. As we strive to re-create the complex material, emotional, and relational productions of our collaborative work history, we seek to give a fuller, denser meaning to it without "being captured by the reflection provided in a single narrative" (Grumet, 1991, p. 72). In this layer then, we organize events and phenomena to create bricolages of understanding where experiences seem sometimes in synch, sometimes in opposition, sometimes in question. It is through and within these multiple accounts that we seek to create an open, polyvalent design rather than a tightly unified discursive pattern. This process helps us make visible those passions and ambiguities, methods and masks that are so much a part of our experience and of that which is "felt, fantasized, and thought— the reality underneath the words, events, and schedules" of our working lives together (Pinar, 1988, p. 139).

Collaboration Is a Cultural and Political Entity

Since we believe "collaboration" does not convey the same meaning for everyone and for all time, but rather functions provisionally within a social and historical context, we take its meaning as open to name and transformation, always variously reconstructed in place and time according to social, personal, and epistemological need. This recognition underscores the contingencies inherent in acts of collaboration. This book functions as an example of such need, and we provide here examples of positive ways of examining collaboration in contexts that are meaningful to us and that we hope will be valuable for others to use and think about.

Linked to this are other important considerations. As we have discovered through our work together, the dimensions of the collaborative experience are far more subtle, spontaneous, and anarchic than we initially imagined. Their various matrices and glare, silences and statements demand complex, inventive response. Thus our collaborations and their representations are situated within the context of critical postmodernism "as a part of a broader pedagogical project which reasserts the primacy of the political while simultaneously engaging the most progressive aspects of modernism" (Giroux, et al., 1996, p. 64). So we assert here the necessity of creating a textual disruption of the conventional modes of discursive production as a politics of production, since "not only the *state* and its *institutions* are terrains of political struggle; [but] so is *language*" (Casey, 1993, p. 158, original italics). Breaking down separations between the various spheres of private and public dialogue; crossing borders between objective and subjective space; and integrating cognitive and intuitive experience in new and different ways are crucial parts of such "broader pedagogical project[s]"; and we view such struggle as a form of political activism. Making decisions about how to express these complex associations in specific form is to also struggle with identifying those forces which constrain or promote human imagination—and, therefore, restrain or enable social transformation.

It is through these processes that some of the complicated phenomena of how individuals make and remake themselves in everyday interaction with each other are brought to consciousness and are thus made concrete in the social world. So the representations of these experiences involve analytic shifts, inventions, and intertexts, not as examples of textual or aesthetic transgression, but as part of our commitment to further exploring the political dimensions of education and identity, of the circuits of power embedded in collaboration and research production, of our loyalties and struggles and hope. If such inquiry (both as experience and as representation) seems unsettling, Michael Apple (1994) reminds us, after all, that "certain things need to be unsettled, need to be shaken . . . [and] for those of us in education, among the most important assumptions that deserve to be 'unsettled' is the belief that research—as it is currently done in both its quantitative and qualitative forms—is a good thing" (p. ix).

* * *

Afterword

May 1, 1998. When we began working together so many years ago, we didn't really anticipate what the process would be like or where it would take us. We did not expect that it wouldn't always be logical. We did not expect that it wouldn't always be fair. We did not expect that it wouldn't always turn out wonderfully—like the romances of our dreams. The reality has, indeed, been tougher. Much tougher. Having traversed the many layers of our work together, we now find ourselves even less certain than we were at the beginning about where we will go next or what we will do. To learn is a part of it. To change is a part of it. To lose is a part of it. Reorganizing everything over and over and over again is a part of it. The whole uneven path that we scramble our way along together is a part of it, even as we struggle to remain a part of it, too.

Chapter Two

Commitment's Tale
(Long Version)

We began working together in 1974. At that time, we were in our mid-twenties, teaching as a two-person education department in a small liberal arts college in southern Wisconsin. Our responsibilities ranged across elementary and secondary undergraduate teacher preparation programs and included foundations courses and field placements, teaching methods and curriculum theory. We supervised student teachers at all levels. We were responsible for the administrative management of the program and the concomitant concerns with ensuring appropriate preparation for state teacher certification for our students and with meeting state program requirements. We both had previously earned our masters degrees in   **(N: All those paths taken and abandoned, methodologies   current**

This chapter's variant form (and in which references are included as text) was produced by chance through the processing of a text scanner intruding its own force. The format of this section is intentional.

and discarded,   identities

shaped and blasted away, all those words

that wear aw

ay over time. What's the

ir

connection with research?)

education at the University of Wisconsin and, before
that, had taught in elementary and secondary schools in this country and
abroad. Our undergraduate preparation included coursework in literature,
language study, the humanities, and the arts. Surprised, but also delighted, by
many of the parallels in our backgrounds, we worked together in the college's
teacher education program, taking

When we work now, we   (J: Does there always
don't know where we're   need to be?
,go;ing tn @@@ @ˆ, @v@ Leigh Gilmore (1994) suggests
  @ "i,'   @ and   that "autobiography
                                   (personal history?)
                              wraps up the interrupted and
fragmentary discourse of identity,   those stories we tell
ourselves and   are told, which hold us together
                    as persons" (p.17).

up wi'th something very different. We begin
with an idea that interests us, but very
quickly it becomes many ideas. It splits
apart i . nto pieces. We split a part into
pie ces. Our one idea becomes a kind of

jum b le. It exp lodes into something like a monkey puzz le, a cactus.   *We*
       become a
cactus to ourselves. If we look carefully,
we can sometimes recognize our competing
assurances about research, our various political and conceptual motivations, our
different senses of self, and our fears which we want and don't want to say. So there's
an idea which almost
z .–im?d:'ately becomes an
*I .*mpossibili'ty. *A* **tangle** of
i *.nte–rnal logic. Systems of*
   competing voice. **Inner** *and* **Outer** *space.*
And then long moments of silence when we wonder how
 to put things

                    together now?

pleasure in our growing collaborations with each other across intellectual, instructional, and personal space. Drawing on our undergraduate backgrounds in literature in particular, and on our initial encounters with educators such as Herbert Read (1943), Maxine Greene (1973), and Herbert Marcuse (1964), whose work spoke differently, but compellingly, about the imperative of incorporating fiction, poetry, and the varied arts in educational practice, we struggled to make spaces in the college's education curriculum for works of the literary imagination. Along with the standard "academic" readings in our courses, we assigned works such as Doris Lessing's *Martha Quest*, John Hersey's *The Child Buyer*, Piri Thomas's *Down These Mean Streets*, and Ray Bradbury's *Dandelion Wine*. Reading these works moved us to think, and to love thinking beyond the literal. We thought our students might be moved by this, too. It was in some of these ways and during many of these shared professional activities that we became friends.

across the wine-dark Valentine sea

Although there was hardly any way to fully recognize it at the time, these experiences provided us with some of the most enduring lessons of our lives. We learned about the real lives of our students as they struggled to "fit" into the adult world of schools and we learned about ourselves. We spent an incredible amount of time together both in and out of school. We worked with the local Head Start agency. We traded books, records, and

 ["**Against the empty, continuous, quantified, infinite time**
of vulgar historicism must be set the full,   **broken, indivisible and**
perfect time of concrete human experience; instead of   **the**
chronological time of pseudo-history,   **the cairological time of**
authentic history;
in place of the total
social process of a dialectic lost in time, the   **interruption**   **and**
immedicacy of dialectic at a standstill . . ." (Giorgio Agamben, 1993, p.
148)].

ideas about teaching. We often ate dinner together at each other's house. We drank the best beer we could afford at the Parkside (a local bar and grill just down the street from our offices at the college). We frequently talked into the early morning hours about love, sex, relationships (in our particular cases, a pending divorce, a breakup with a longtime girlfriend earlier that year), about the impact on our lives of both our mothers' recent deaths, about writing and writers. (We discovered that we were reading many of the same authors: Doris Lessing, Elizabeth Bishop, Sylvia Plath, Roland Barthes.) We simply took as a given the redemptive power of art (an assumption we both had, at that time in our lives, little reason to doubt).

Then, in August, two weeks before the 1975 academic year was to begin, one of us (Jan) abruptly resigned, sold her house, and moved to Madison with her two young daughters. The suddenness of this decision left Nick feeling stunned, betrayed.

> (J: And Sidonie Smith (1993) says that
> "autobiographical writing is always a gesture toward publicity,
> displaying toward an impersonal public an individual's
> interpretation of experience" (p. 159) as mixed up
> as it may be.)

Anger.   Disappointment.   Confusion.
           "Who are you anyway?

Where are you from in my life?

       What sort
of identity are you?

Later that year, Jan bought a house on Westlawn near Lake Wingra and became a substitute teacher; the next year she began working at the University of Wisconsin as a research assistant.

       . . . and why?"

Nick taught until June, picking up most of Jan's college responsibilities, then began to work for Armco Steel. In 1977, he began teaching English in the University of Wisconsin Center System and helped establish a program for students from low-income backgrounds who wanted to pursue education beyond high school.

By 1980, we had each returned to graduate school at the University of Wisconsin to complete our doctoral work in education. Over the intervening years, we had maintained an irregular contact, mostly sharing the progressions (regressions?) of our (hyper-chaotic) personal lives. But now living near each other again, in the same neighborhood, we resumed our engagement with our professional studies. While our areas of formal academic inquiry focused on different aspects of curriculum at the early childhood and primary levels, we also continued to read and work independently and then together again on multiple artistic, cultural, and literary projects within and outside the academy. At the time, we weren't actively connecting these projects in any defined way to issues of curriculum or to a clearly articulated research agenda. We just didn't imagine that art and curriculum, research and experience could be integrated in any meaningful way; so in the carved-out microspaces of "real life," Nick continued to paint; Jan raised her kids.

our admz'ration for the thinking of Thomas Bernhard. – "Since my grandfather the poet ZS dead, I now had the 'right to write and I used the entire world, transforming it I . nto poems."

But Madison was extremely important because it put us in daily contact with a committed group of educators and individuals who were actively engaged in exploring/studying the promises (and the predicaments) of creating alternative forms of knowledge, alternative ways of learning. Some of these friends and teachers made spaces in their courses for the examination (and creation) of "imaginative forms of difference" before such practice had a name. We were introduced to the works of Michel Foucault, Jacques Derrida, and Helene Cixous. We began to struggle with what their thinking might mean for doing educational research. Partly because of these influences, Nick returned again to his earlier readings of the surrealist writers, such as Max Ernst, Raoul Hausmann, Gertrude Stein, and Kurt Schwitters, finding in them a historical base for studying the avant-garde children's books of Harlin Quist, his dissertation topic. Jan struggled to integrate feminist, critical, postmodern theory with the daily realities of being a student, a teacher, a mother. We began again to spend more time together, discussing our understandings of these authors and what we were trying to do in our own work. Even though we weren't confident to integrate their thinking into our dissertations with the force we would have wished, they began to exert an unconscious power in the shaping of our ideas about teaching and learning, thinking and writing.

After receiving our doctorates, we continued/resumed teaching foundations and educational methods courses, but at new positions in

> (N: Are academic researchers, as Donmoyer (1996) suggests, "permitted to advance all sorts of nontraditional ideas, [but] ...expected to do this in relatively traditional ways, that is, in a way we have come to recognize as academic as opposed to some other form of discourse" (p. 20)?

We work in fits and starts. No line. No ending. No thought   anymore

> *of proof, of validi 'y, of explanation,*

(N: In his assessment of narrative's revival across disciplines, Bill Buford (1996) points out, "narrative writing is, at its most elementary, an act of seduction: its object is arousal. It arouses a curiosity, an interest, an expectation. It flirts with the reader, stimulates an appetite, verges on satisfying it, only to stimulate another, even greater appetite" (p. 12).

> *of being good. Separated by geography, economic@ family and work schedules, personal history, and even the shape of our own strange dreams, we feel that we are nevertheless connected. Sometimes we think that we admire our friendship more than the act Of writing itself* (J: Madeline Grumet

Our

(1991) writes that "our
work does not start with   stories are masks
theory, *but always with*   through which we
something else.
Is it   can be seen, and with
love?

every telling we stop
the flood and swirl of thought
so someone can get a glimpse of us,

and maybe catch us if they can" (p. 69).

geographically distanced institutions (Jan at the University of Oregon; Nick at Smith College). Like most other newly appointed assistant professors, we also began to construct our research and publication agendas. One of us initiated a series of research explorations, examining curricular decision making and relational aspects of teacher-student interactions (Jan). The other pursued questions of how art and the literary imagination are issues for education, examining instances of the avant-garde in children's literature as sites of political resistance and curricular reformulation (Nick).

In 1988, we undertook our initial collaborative research project, "The Selective Tradition in Teachers' Choice of Children's Literature: Does It Exist in the Elementary Classroom?", a yearlong study of elementary teachers' independent literary selections for classroom use and the dynamics of their curricular decision-making. At that time, we were both still very much concerned with issues related to the possibilities (and the predicaments) inherent in our previous work with literature and curriculum, particularly its political and positional dynamics mediated by practicing teachers in actual classrooms. Working from a theoretical background that made imperative the critical examination of texts (both assigned and trade) as a site for the construction of curricular knowledge and classroom practice, as well as from our intertwined personal and collaborative histories, we were especially interested in these issues as they related to the argument of the selective tradition. This notion, that books are not ideologically neutral objects, that they both reflect and convey specific sets of sociocultural values, beliefs, and attitudes to their readers, made sense to us. We saw   (N: **Buford also tells us that "stories also protect us from chaos . . . that they are a fundamental unit of knowledge, the foundation of memory,**

essential to the way we make sense of our lives . . . We have returned to narratives . . . in many fields of knowledge. . . because it is impossible to live without them" (1996, p. 12).

When we work now, we are all over the place. Logic is an inferno that feeds us i . n the roar of its mind. Edging down the path, feeling its blaze on our eyes and faces, we move on. There's a map that someone gave us once. Where did we leave it? The phone rings and rings and rings n obvious places, but we've tried to train ourselves to listen for other things. Rings of what?

   (N: **A kind of stumbling whose meaning is neither immune nor clear.**)

When we work now, we try to find colorings in our w rit In g s that w e abandoned so long ago (in the lives we abandoned so long ago.). Finish is no longer anything.   Stopping and starting get confused. Direction? We did that. Leave everything rough and uneven now so you can see the spaces in between where things don't connect and don't for

ce them. Where your mind struggles to translate what i . t sees anyway. Could that be a practice? Stumbling, along the way, or crawling, we work with whatever occupies us. It can be anything and e–ve r–thing.

Take what you find on your way (or in your way),

and put it there

too.

our efforts partially grounded in the previous theoretical work of Michael
Apple (1980, 1982, 1988); Allan Luke, et al. (1986); Patrick Shannon (1986);
Joel Taxel (1981, 1983); and Raymond Williams (1977); who differently argued
that teachers, as they selected books for classroom use, were essentially
selecting for or against the representations of particular kinds of cultural
experience and value in their classes.   Sensitive to these ideologically
constructed analyses, but startled to find so little research evidence that
supported (or developed) such argumentation at the grounded base of actual
teaching practice, we began the first of our projects on literature and
curriculum.   In addition to providing concrete, vocal evidence for these
ideologically inflected issues, we envisioned our collaborative effort as
potentially contributing to a more culturally inclusive pedagogy.   Our

long distance late
night

collaboration had proceeded smoothly, one of us reviewing literature, another
analyzing the data. Our division of labor seemed to work despite the Oregon-
Massachusetts, space-time, ego-also separations.   In the spring of 1989, we
presented our work together at the annual meeting of the American
Educational Research Association in San Francisco and published it in the
content literature soon afterward (Jipson & Paley, 1991). We were pleased with
the positions we were taking. And we trusted each other's intentions to be the
intentions of each of us individually, as well as both of us together.

During the next year, however, things shifted once again.   Jan moved to
Michigan and then to California when the University of Oregon closed the
program in which she worked; Nick moved to George Washington University

in Washington, D.C. New locations, new jobs, new turbulence: continued pressure to publish, another baby, another girlfriend, another divorce. How to write, how to even think, when chaos is the norm? Tremendous pressures were placed on our friendship. Our work continued under terrific stress and developed an authority of its own.

It was partly within this intensified context, that our next three studies, "Is There a Base to Today's Literature–Based Reading Programs?", "Fiction as Curricular Text," and "Literature/Curriculum/Authority/Absence: A Parallel Conversation" emerged the way they did (Jipson & Paley, 1992a, 1992b, 1994). Increasingly sensitized to the role of the personal in cultural and educational analysis, we chose to look at the dynamics of

(J: I used to read theory: Foucault, Gramsci, Bakhtin, but now I am attracted to astrology, the writings of priests and mystics. And the stories of children.)

decision making from more narrative and autobiographical perspectives. This representational standpoint mirrored our conceptual repositioning away from a theoretical perspective substantially based on neo-Marxist analysis. We found ourselves, instead, moving toward representations of these questions from a progressively more dialogic series of personal reflections about the status of literature in the formation of identity, teacher agency, and classroom pedagogy. We interviewed colleagues, students, friends, and each other. Working long distance became difficult (intolerable, it seemed); our phone bills erupted, and we began a series of cross-country trips to develop and refine our drafts. Visiting each other continued the collaboration on a personal level. The narrative nature of our work demanded face to face interaction. We began to argue about words, inflections, intent and found that we were moving beyond description, chased by nuance and intuition. We worried about whether our work violated the conventions of objectivity and neutrality, and we spent long hours discussing what this and our work represented in each of our lives. No easy answers here. No really easy answers anywhere, anymore.

Curriculum's inner force,

In retrospect,

         (N: "that, from some distance, someone might have
thought I was making a fire in my hands"
                                    G. Soto, 1990, p. 24).

When we work now, there are bills to pay; still we are I . ntrigued by the functions of chance and the unconscious Where did we first read about that and forget? **Love letters** *we've saved remind us of their powerful radiance. Or certain (parts og poems. Long ago, one of us remembers* **(it was in high school), reading Rilke and how that head–on collision** *bashed at the doors of our ;heart. When did we forget I . ts all–out war for our whole spz'rit? For the existence of Possibilities?*

                    Adrienne Rich wrote " . . . to teach you names
                                                for things
                                        you did not need . . . "

we now acknowledge that this theoretic shift from the established traditions of analytic representations to representations reflecting multiple relational, contextual standpoints and voices may have risked the unintentional consequence of not clearing political terrain by providing descriptions of a "specific road" ahead for teachers struggling with issues of text selection and curricular decision-making.   Still, we sensed that this representational movement contributed to the reformulation of research politics from other important directions. Acknowledging (and extending) the influence that fiction has held in furthering our own understanding of ourselves and our educational practice, and responding to the imperatives articulated by feminist and narrative theorizing to repoliticize thinking about literature and curriculum through testimony and self-articulation (Ashton-Warner, 1963; Felman & Laub, 1992; Gilmore; 1994, hooks, 1994; Smith, 1993), we sought to integrate these forms of discourse into systems of already constituted analytic knowledge, teaching and research.

   (J: **"Stories are all that we can ever have; stories compounded out of the stories we re–tell to ourselves and to others; stories our caregivers and others told to and tell us; and stories woven around the odd artifact we have retained (like family photos, pictures we drew or a battered teddy still sitting in the cupboard.")**
     (Stainton Rogers, 1992, p. 19)

 This was hard work, and sometimes it got really intense working together. We were tired, impatient, frequently irritated with the different directions (inner and outer) each of our lives seemed to be taking. During a visit to Washington in June 1992, we decided to work on a book that would integrate our formalized research projects with the responses of colleagues from other universities, from the public schools, and from our classes; we initially gave it the name "Collaboration and Critique." We spent over a year on this project, and then two more years watching it fall apart. Somehow, it just didn't work the way we wanted. We weren't working the way we wanted. Who knows why? Was it because Jan was finishing another book with other people? Was it because Nick's effort was being pulled away by a family illness back in the Midwest? Was it because we were no longer so sure of each other's intentions? Writing became very difficult. We blamed each other, and then, we each blamed ourselves. All that thinking and rethinking, writing and rewriting, going nowhere.

(J: There is always possibility; there is always starting again.)

   Nowhere is where you sometimes find yourself beginning all over again. Jan
didn't want to give the book up; she felt she owed it to her friends and
colleagues who contributed their energy and ideas to the project. Nick didn't
want to give it up either; despite all the tracings and erasings, differences and
disarray. Method? Reworking things over and over again, adding or scraping
away whatever was needed in order to make sense of the work involved. Jan:
How did we get so involved in all this?

It was a long time ago.
You were working without wings
In the changing time
Falling to the ground
Turning yourself into oak leaves
Making pictures and reasons
For me.

In that time
Weather fed on the ground.
And I'd turn around
To anything you wanted to be.
Sometimes, this
Made sounds in my head.
In one, I heard an afterlife
Beyond you
Crystallizing in my hand.
In another, a little animal
Was giving thanks
For not starving yet.

What can we really know?
What dare we really see?

Peel the layers back
One by one
What will the windows say?

Maybe in the afterward
There'll be a map of how
Everything keeps grinding together.
One more picture
Taken from another
Side of the world. Since

these initial studies, we have continued to examine other questions related to the place of literature in educational settings. But now our newer work is even more different. Still sensitive to, yet less constrained by, the weight of both institutional research and our own traditions of research representation, we find ourselves increasingly immersed in our attention to the substantial, important work in the different modes of feminist, postmodern, and art theorizing, especially as such theorizing is articulated as
critical

(N: What is this voice?)

*When we work now, similarities never compete. We scrounge. We descend. We get
turned around and when we put something down, we wonder.– OK, this so
mething next to that something next to that something. What do we see? What is
that **image telling us? We** try to
fill our little beach pails with all the sea and sand we could never quite get in them
so many summers ago. Sometimes it's so easy now, and sometimes it's hard. Sand
and sea. Scrounging and sleep. Scroungz'ng for a rose that grows
out of **the roc,@.** Or z . s it the other way around? Scrounging for a way on our
way. All you have
to do*

is choose.
When we work now.

Educated in another's In z distant country,

we were fortunate to lose our way back.   Sometimes we get a glimpse of it as we turn
corners, and we're getti . n g better a t cutting across cou n try.
 Dreams help. But sometimes a dream is like a 'reflection you didn't expect. The
reflectzon of a surprise you once felt about learning things you really liked. Or
the reflection that told you what you didn@t want to know. W indowz dear as
daughters! How they took you by surprise.

Or was it a cyclone?

Expectation and tradition?

Competition, envy, fear.

Dream, risk, power.

Whose ideas were we anyway?

Windows dear as daughters.

(Were they ?)

practice (Aronowitz & Giroux, 1991; Becker, 1994; Deleuze & Guattari, 1987;
DuPlessis, 1990; Lather, 1991; Trinh, 1991, 1992).   It is in our shared
appreciation for this contemporary work that challenges analytic
representations grounded in forms of unified narrative, linear thinking, and

objective voice that we now find another base. Drawing support from and sympathetic to these critical explorations, many of which are as much works of art as projects of social and cultural criticism, we've begun to experiment with different ways of encoding "data" in transmittable form. For us, this newer reformulation of our collaborative efforts in recent projects (Jipson & Paley, 1997, 1999; Paley & Jipson, 1995, 1997a, 1997b)

December?   It was January. That crazy day when it was raining so hard in San Francisco, like it always does just after the holidays, and you wonder why   you ever moved out here in the first place, and I looked up from my coffee and croissant at that little shop on the southwest corner of Post and Stockton. "Nick!"   Yelling across the rain. "Sorry! My class got out late, traffic was awful, couldn't make it to the airport, the winds on the damn bridge were phenomenal. Let's have a drink at the St. Francis. Where   have you been?"

"Look at this. I've got a great idea. It finally hit me over the Rockies. Forget C&C. At least for now. We can get back to it. The reviewers were right anyway. Listen: What comes into your mind when you think Daredevil Research?"

Dare what???

has opened up independent, affirmative spaces for a more experimental reframing of questions about literature and curriculum, while we simultaneously explore the possibilities, languages, and writing practices for re/presenting research knowledge today.

What if
"Method:
Who am   I   ?"
                              is   no
longer simply a question
of how, but of how far to go? Does this stake out anything useful?
Example: If we are friends first, first and finally, why can't that
experience, too, become a subject for our inquiry, for our analysis, for
our understanding? To help us better understand *the agendas we make, the*
selves we create in everyday history, the struggles and situations that develop?

The subsequent years brought successes (individual, collaborative) but also
sadness: serious illness in our families, surgery, death. What do these events
have to do with research? No book on method that we know mentions them.
Hard then to believe in some of those philosophies, as good as they are . And
when Jan called out (again): "Nick, I'm drowning,"
what else was there?
              Can there really be

the
possibility of a research about literature and
curriculum that is a challenge to research in
literature and
curriculum? That explores what
Elliot Eisner (1997)   has
identified as "the edges of possibility"
(p. 9) in data representation?   Or that opens up what
Foucault (1988)

              (N: ...or fate?)

When we work

now, we often remember what we were then. When we were I . n love for the second

or third time and not **in**

any *precise way when anyone you*

knew could say that this experience *was the direct result of some dependent or*

independent variable, or an outcome, or a prediction fo

r future research ... We remember how o

ne Saturday afternoon (it was in late March and when by complete **chance**

) we stopped into a gallery off Russell Square to get out of the rain and we saw for the

first time **some** *of the* **z . mpossible** *assemblies of discarded things by Kurt*

Schwitters. How long had

we   *been lost from them?*

We   *were blown away by*

the   **roughn***ess of*

their

thrown away

        power and by the delicateness of their

thrown

away power **and by**

the rough

        ness of our loneliness and the imp

'bilit'es of that t

                                                        (N:
                                                        How
                                                        then to
                                                        teach "sliding up
                                                        and down the scales of

importance, the destruction

of

the scales of importance?"

(DuPlessis, 1990, p.163).

impossi **bI** **spring** *before we came to work*

now.

(J: Teaching remains the most real thing I do...my students give me
back the life I once wanted.)

when we work now, we are seized . by the

accumulation

of days gone by. Notebooks

of solitude. Letters from friends. The

ten moons of

babies. The four moons of stone.

Languages that once existed

somewhere

when we were

in one of his last interviews, called "fracture areas" (pp. 36–37) in established
systems of knowledge and analytical power?

And it still isn't easy. As we continue to

struggle with our own research histories,

our shifting theoretical frameworks, and our

shared commitment to collaborative work,

such questions help us better comprehend

why, "in a moment of decentering, then, of

eroding authorities, of disappearing

absolutes, we have to discover new ways of

going on . . . [ways] that do not duplicate

other

REFERENCES

narratives" (Greene, 1994, pp. 218, 217).

Agamben, G. (1993). *Infancy and history: Essays on the destruction of experience.* London: Verso.

Apple, M.   (1980). *Ideology and curriculum.* Boston: Routledge.

Apple, M.   (1982). *Education and power.* Boston: Routledge.

Apple, M.

(1988). *Teachers and texts: A political economy of class and gender relations in education.* New York: Routledge.

Aronowitz, S. & Giroux, H. (1991). *Postmodern education: Politics, culture, and* social   *criticism.* Minneapolis: University of Minnesota Press.

Becker, C. (ed.). (1994). *The subversive imagination: Artists, society, and social responsibility.* New York: Routledge.

Buford, B. (1996). The seduction of storytelling: Why is narrative suddenly so popular?   *The New Yorker (June 24 & July 1, 1996),* 11–12.

young. The one hundred eighty-se,ven oceans ofgold. Now we find pulses in symbols that we never

i@k   new   e,–

xiste@i. **@Vl@lere id**

they come

from?

Deleuze, G. & Guattari, F. (1987). A thousand plateaus (B. Massumi, Trans.). Minneapolis: University of Minnesota Press.

Donmoyer, R.   (1996). Educational research in an era of paradigm proliferation: What's a journal editor to do? *Educational Researcher 25* (2), 19–25.

DuPlessis, R. (1990). *The pink guitar: Writing as feminist practice.* New York: Routledge.

Eisner, E. (1997). The promise and perils of alternative forms of data representation. *Educational Researcher 26* (6), 4–10.

Felman, S. & Laub, M. (1992). *Testimony: Crises of witnessing in literature, psychoanalysis,   and history.* New York: Routledge.

Foucault, M. (1988). *Politics, philosophy, culture: Interviews and other writings 1977–1984* (L. Kritzman, Trans.). New York: Routledge.

Gilmore, L. (1994). *Autobiographics: A feminist theory of women's self-representation.*
    Ithaca, NY: Cornell University Press.

Greene, M. (1973). *Teacher as stranger: Educational philosophy for the modern age.* Belmont, CA: Wadsworth.

(1994). Postmodernism and the crisis of representation. *English Education 26* (4), 206–219.

Grumet, M. (1991). The politics of personal knowledge. In C. Witherell & N. Noddings (Eds.), *Stories lives tell: Narrative and dialogue in education.* New York: Teachers College Press.

When we work now, no top, no bottom. No back, no front No under, no over, no symmetry. No yard we own. Heap ideas on top of ideas until they give us their own shape anywhere. Sometimes this can be **startling** *–sometimes a m ess. Sometimes this results in a hunger for something we can@t name. The idea of heaps obsesses us. Their ridiculous shape. Refusing organization. Refusing to be a building. Refusing their destz'ny to be an architecture. Their density is what really attracts us. We* **often wonder now***: What else possibly could?*

hooks, b. (1994). *Teaching to transgress: Education as the practice of freedom.*
New York: Routledge.

Jipson, J. & Paley, N. (1991). The selective tradition in teachers' choice of children's
literature: Does it exist in the elementary classroom? *English Education 23* (3),   148–159.

Jipson, J. & Paley, N. (1992a). Is there a base to today's literature–based reading programs? *English Education 24* (2), 77–90.

Jipson, J. & Paley, N. (1992b). Fiction as curricular text. Educational Foundations 6 (2), 21–33.

Jipson, J. & Paley, N. (1994). Literature/curriculum/authority/absence: A parallel
conversation. *English Education 26* (4), 220–235.

Jipson, J. & Paley, N. (1997). *Daredevil research: Re-creating analytic practice.*
New York: Peter Lang .

Jipson, J. & Paley, N. (1999). Animals and
curriculum masters. In C. T. P.Diamond &
C.
Mullen (Eds.), *The postmodern educator:*
Arts-based inquiries and teacher development.
New York: Peter Lang.

Lather, P. (1991*). Getting smart: Feminist research and pedagogy with/in the*
postmodern. New York: Routledge.

Luke, A., Cooke, J. & Luke, C. (1986). The selective tradition in action:
          Gender bias in   student teachers' selections of children's literature.
English Education 18 (4), 209–   218.

When we work now, we're ti'red of little sentences and
big sentences and paragraphs and conclusions. We like pretexts. (Pre-texts?) We're
surprised by beauty's renewal in these kinds of forms when there's still no official name
for it. Or norm. We're surprised about how their small cyclones blow us away
when we work now. We still get surprised at how easily we can still be eaten alive and
how that relates to everything else in its own
undefined ways
..and again (from the W-reck).of –
tell it over and over,
the words thick with unmeaning –yet
never have we been closer

to the truth of the lies we were living... FY

Marcuse, H. (1964*). One dimensional man.* Boston: Beacon Press.

Paley, N. & Jipson, J. (1995, April*).
Research, repetition, anti-memory: A
reexamination of the selective tradition in
teachers' choice of children's literature.* An
electronic research performance presented
at the annual meeting of the American
Educational Research Association, San
Francisco, CA.

Paley, N., & Jipson, J. (1997a) Duplications. *Taboo: The Journal of Culture and
Education 2* (2), 269.

Paley, N., & Jipson, J. (1997b). Personal history: Reseaching literature and
curriculum (literal, alter, hyper). *English Education 29* (1), 59–70.
Read, H. (1943). *Education through art.* London: Faber and Faber.

Shannon, P. (1986). Hidden within the
pages: A study of social perspective in
young children's favorite books.
The Reading Teacher 39 (7), 656–663.

Smith, S. (1993). *Subjectivity, identity and the body: Women's autobiographical
practices in the twentieth century.* Bloomington, IN: Indiana University Press.
Soto, G. (1990). *A Fire In My Hands.* New York:
Scholastic.

Stainton-Rogers, R. & W. (1992*). Stories of childhood: Shifting agendas of child
concern.*
Toronto: University of

TorontoPress.

Taxel, J. (1981). The outsiders of the American revolution: The selective
tradition in   children's fiction. *Interchange in Educational Policy 12* (2–3),
206–228.

Taxel, J. (1983). The American revolution in children's fiction. *Research in the
Teaching of English 17* (1), 61–83.

Trinh, M. (1991). *When the moon
waxes red: Representation, gender, and cultural   politics.* New York:
Routledge.

Trinh, M. (1992). *Framer framed_.* New York: Routledge.

Williams, R. (1977). *Marxism and literature.* Oxford: Oxford University Press.
*When we work now, what else is there? We're
tumbling. Deep snow? A
deadline to meet?   An
endless   column that*
remz'nds   us of
the endle.ss
way to   go? Is there a
lesson to **learn** *or teach?   Can you*

*really hear
        the words? The format?*

*The whole
production?*

(through our
numbness, can we **ever really hear** *the*
words??)

When *we work now, everything* **chan ges witho**

ut *letting us know. It gets harder and harder to bear.*
l@– gets harder an
d 'harder –0
stop. *it gets harder and*
harder to know.
When we work now, we can often feel our hands
navigating like faces.– No shorelines

(This is commitment, too.)

Santa Rosa, California

Commentary 1: Ruptures

Commitment's Tale (Long Version)

It is only in the rupturing of the hegemonic narrative of modernity that we can reclaim research and research presentation as a site for all to access and engage. Paulo Freire (1998) has taught us to stand against the narrowness of thought and selective practices that defend the preservation of exclusive talk. He has cautioned that "there are no values of which we cannot speak, no areas in which one must remain silent" (p. 58). This helps open the way for many different kinds of conversations to be heard. Talk reflecting personal or intimate concerns may emerge at any time and anywhere, and its languages may be all tangled up in the stuff of dreamy, edgy, or puzzling experiences. But this development may also create a kind of "open source" research in which everyone or anyone can participate.

In this collection of our collaborative work, we confront research traditions which have served to alienate individuals from their own concerns, their own languages, and their own struggles to name— in ways that are meaningful to them— the complex, often asynchronous tensions that shape their lives. We see this practice as a crucial step in the larger pedagogical process of reconstructing the terms of how individuals are allowed to critically read the world and their situation in it. So through examples of our own work we hope to disrupt the conventions that have defined educational research for many decades. But a major question remains: How do we sidestep the equally alienating discourses of postmodern theory?

As we write here not only of our collaborative efforts, but also of our work as an on-going struggle to free ourselves from forms of inquiry and discourse that forbid the shape of our dreams, understandings, and hope— have we fallen, however, into the same trap that we have critiqued? At times, our collaborations have been identified as "postmodern," and we have struggled with the implications of this term. We have re-considered what others have pointed to as the potentially distancing effects of postmodern practice— the mystifications of postmodern theorizing, the sometimes disconnected, fragmented identification of data for analysis, and issues of intelligibility within the frequently disruptive styles of experimental modes of data display. In "exercis[ing] the right to our [own] curiosity" (Freire, 1998, p. 60), and in attempting to affirm the authenticity of our own voices and the specific contexts within which they have found meaning and shape, have we also created new structures that obscure and frustrate in a different way? Do our experimentations with genre/generic formulation actually reproduce the same exclusionary traditions? Are there really (no) boundaries to what can be said and understood, to what can be named and how?

Chapter Three

The Selective Tradition in Teachers' Choice of Children's Literature: Does It Exist in the Elementary Classroom?

Choosing a children's book for classroom use seems like one of the easiest curricular decisions a teacher can make. At first glance, the procedure appears to involve little more than choosing a well-known, well-liked, or well-recommended text for a given grade level. The matter is not so simple, however; and at the moment, teachers' selection of children's books for classroom use is attracting as much attention and controversy as any other issue in reading and language arts education.

Much of this attention is the result of recent work by a diverse group of educational sociologists, curriculum specialists, and literary theorists who have described a "selective tradition" in books and teachers' choice of literature in instructional settings (Apple, 1980, 1982; Dixon, 1977; Fetterley, 1978; Shannon, 1986; Taxel, 1981, 1983; Wald, 1981; Williams, 1977).

According to these educators, books are not ideologically neutral objects; that is, they both reflect and convey certain sets of sociocultural values, beliefs, and attitudes to their readers. These educators also believe that because of this, book choice is a weighted procedure, since the very process of choosing certain literary works for classroom use involves the simultaneous exclusion of others. Thus, teachers, as they make their book choices, essentially "select" for or against the existence of such cultural values in their classrooms. In describing the nature of this selective process further, these educators argue that too frequently such choices tend to disregard or exclude literary works for school study that are by and about women, people of color or ethnic minority background, and certain social classes, in favor of books featuring predominately white, Euro-American, male authors and subjects. They conclude their argument by submitting that such selection diminishes the legitimacy of one group in favor of another and presents students with an ideologically biased, culturally exclusive, and ultimately false view of society.

This process of selection/exclusion has crucial implications for classroom teachers today, given recent curricular developments in reading and language arts education. In many school districts, for example, more and more teachers are increasingly entrusted with the responsibility of designing literature-based reading/literacy programs, a process that involves the identification and selection of works of fiction, drama, poetry, and nonfiction for course use. Other teachers are becoming actively involved in selecting literature for use as part of innovative curricula that cross content areas. Such programs of study currently integrate literature in disciplines outside the reading/English classroom as early as the primary grades through the graduate level (Coles, 1989; Page, 1988). As teacher choice of literature assumes a more influential role in school study programs, the issues surrounding the process of selection/exclusion become even more pivotal and warrant careful attention.

Regrettably, despite the extensive theoretical groundwork describing the outlines of the selective tradition over the past few years, virtually no research has investigated how, or if, this process actually operates in teachers' choice of literary works for classroom use. This oversight is especially noticeable at the elementary level. In the only empirical study to date, Luke, Cooke, and Luke (1986) asked fifty-six Australian student teachers to select a single children's book that they liked and that they thought primary school children would like and benefit from. Analysis of book choices indicated that "most students had not considered gender or race of author or character in their selections at all" (p. 214) and that student teachers' selections were "predominantly written by and about Anglo-European males, and the characterization of male and female characters was extremely conventional and stereotypical" (p. 213). As a result of these findings, they conclude that, "[i]n all, the survey results indicate unconscious gender and racial bias in student teachers' commonsense assumptions about 'what's appropriate for kids to read'" (p. 216) and "that too often the cultural/curricular selection process entails a naive, acritical adoption of texts which risks perpetuating the 'minimization, distortion, and outright exclusion' of the experience of women, particular social classes, and ethnic minorities" (p. 216).

While Luke, Cooke, and Luke (1986) provide initial empirical evidence to support the view that a selective tradition exists at the elementary level, they do so only on the basis of data gathered from preservice teachers, a group unfortunately lacking in actual classroom experience and practice; characteristics which may well inform and shape literary judgment, selection, and taste. In reviewing their study, we wondered if inservice elementary teachers in "real" schools would also choose literary works which predominately feature white, Euro-American, male authors and subjects. We also wondered if practicing teachers would exhibit the same acritical attitudes of book selection as their less-experienced counterparts when asked to identify their reasons for selecting a particular children's book for classroom use.

Design

In order to explore possible answers to these questions, we asked public and independent elementary school teachers from urban, suburban, and rural settings in Massachusetts, Wisconsin, and Oregon if they would like to participate in a study intended to increase understanding of the use of children's books in elementary school classrooms. Fifty-five women teachers from two schools in each state agreed to participate, twenty from

Massachusetts, seventeen from Wisconsin, and eighteen from Oregon. The average number of years of elementary classroom experience for these teachers was twelve-and-one-half years, with a range of from one to forty years of teaching experience. The sample included two kindergarten teachers, one seventh grade teacher, and from eight to ten teachers in each grade, one through six.

We developed a questionnaire to elicit information about book choices from participating teachers in a clear and straightforward manner. Recognizing the hectic and demanding schedule of elementary school teachers, we asked them simply to name the titles, authors, and main characters of three children's books that they had used in their classrooms during the past year and state their reasons for selecting each book for use in their class. Our goal was to obtain a small sample of book choices for each teacher which would reflect their personal preferences. We did not ask them to report the most recent books used in their classroom, books mandated by their curriculum, or their favorite books, preferring that teachers make their own decisions about what books were important to include. This procedure permitted teachers to conceptualize and construct rationales for their choices, thus reflecting their personal beliefs about using children's books.

The questionnaires were distributed to participating teachers at their schools in spring 1988, and they were asked to return them directly to the researchers.

Data Analysis

Initial data analysis involved our independently sorting the books listed by the teachers according to author's name. In a similar way, each author's and main character's sex and ethnic background was coded. Poetry books, information books without human characters, and animal stories with main characters of unspecified sex or ethnic background were coded as separate categories. In cases of inter-coder disagreement, discussion continued until agreement was reached. In several cases, we solicited the outside expertise of a children's librarian and a professor of children's literature to resolve questions.

Coding of reasons for selecting each of the books was completed by sorting questionnaires for each of the books named according to apparently similar explanations. Three general categories of reasons emerged from this process, each of which will be discussed in detail in the following section.

Findings and Discussion

Overall, teachers selected a total of 155 books, representing 104 different authors. Several books were named more than once, and several authors were represented by more than one book. Of the 104 authors named in our study, 57 (55 percent) were male. These male authors accounted for 91 (59 percent) of the 155 books listed by the teachers surveyed, a percentage identical to that found by Luke, Cooke, and Luke (1986) in their study of student teachers in Australia. In addition, 99 (95 percent) of the authors named were of Euro-American heritage. Only 5 of the chosen authors were from ethnic minorities.

With regard to gender and cultural background of main characters in the books, 32 of the 155 books chosen were either information books without human characters (11), animal stories with main characters of undetermined sex (16), or poetry collections (5). Of the 123 remaining books with identifiable main characters, the majority (80, or 65 percent) featured males as primary book characters. The representation of cultural diversity among main characters in the books selected was even more limited. Of the 123 books with identifiable main characters, only 8 (6 percent) included main characters from North American minority cultures; this number included 4 Black, 3 Native American, and 1 Japanese-American main character.

In discussing this data one can, of course, take the position that these figures and percentages merely reflect the relative availability of books by and about male and female authors and subjects of different cultural backgrounds in the school districts of teachers surveyed. One can also argue, however, that the data suggests that experienced teachers are not taking full advantage of those books which are increasingly being published which are by and about women and people from culturally diverse backgrounds. Whatever the case, when tabulated quantitatively, the results from our survey of inservice elementary school teachers clearly confirm the findings by Luke, Cooke, and Luke and offer empirical support for the existence of a selective tradition in elementary teachers' choice of children's literature for use in contemporary American classrooms.

A much more complex and dynamic picture emerges from the data in this study, however, when one looks beyond simple numerical tabulation of book choices and begins to review the reasons teachers gave for selecting the books they did. We found that the teachers in this study offered a variety of reasons for adopting particular books. In order to fully explore these multiple reasons, we considered in this analysis all the books named, whether or not they had an identifiable main character.

In all, teachers gave 170 reasons for selecting particular books. Several teachers offered multiple explanations for selecting a given text, thus generating a greater number of reasons for choosing the 155 books. (When multiple rationales were offered, they were coded in each relevant category.) We found that the many reasons listed by the teachers could be summarized in three major categories of response. Teachers selected books because of (1) the appropriateness of the text within a larger instructional context, (2) personal preference for the book because of the story, author, illustrations, or award-winning status, and (3) the recognition of gender, race, and ethnicity as important elements in the book selection process. In the following sections, we further explore each of these categories, providing selected responses of teachers themselves in order to reveal the thought and reasoning underlying the decisions they made.

1. Instructional/Curricular Factors

The importance of selecting a children's book within a larger instructional context was the primary reason teachers gave for choosing the books they did, mentioning this factor seventy-nine times. This category included two somewhat overlapping groups: one relating book choice to unit content (thirty-seven comments, or 22 percent), the other relating book choice to a specific curricular skill (forty-two comments, or 25 percent).

In the former group, some teachers were very succinct in describing the book selection process. A fourth grade teacher explained her line of reasoning for choosing the book, *How to Eat Fried Worms*, "It fits well into my predicting consequences health unit." A kindergarten teacher commented on her choice of *The Very Hungry Caterpillar*, "We have been studying the life cycle of the caterpillar. We started with caterpillars, then cocoons, and finally beautiful butterflies. The story tied in beautifully."

Several of the teachers provided more extensive commentary, their responses reflecting attempts to integrate children's literature within unit material. For example, a second grade teacher described how she integrated two children's books into her science unit on oceans in order to provide her students with a richer framework for appreciating and discussing unit content and to show the interconnectedness and caring relationships among a community of very different living creatures, "*Swimmy* was excellent for an ocean unit showing survival and working together. Several fish swim together in schools to fool larger fish. A discussion and art project followed, using sponge painting and tissue paper." She also reported using *Titus Tidewater* as "another excellent book for the ocean unit. We had just traveled to Mystic [a Connecticut seaport] and learned more about tide pools. This gave children another opportunity to see the other animals in a tide pool but most important it talked about caring and taking care of others."

A fifth grade teacher who selected three children's books, *Roll of Thunder, Hear My Cry*; *Where the Lilies Bloom*; and *The Red Pony* for use in her class's long-term unit on United States regions also chose *Adam of the Road* by Elizabeth Janet Gray for integration into a different thematic unit during the year. She wrote:

This book was chosen for its accurate portrayal of life during the medieval times. The main character loses his father during a fair and has his dog stolen so he must travel alone to many different towns, monasteries, and castles to find them. The novel's flavor of medieval life and use of a child as a main character makes it more relevant to 5th graders. They can more easily associate and compare/contrast life styles, which makes this a good historical fiction choice to be used when we study that time period.

As previously mentioned, forty-two teachers chose a particular children's book because it provided a richer, more contextually meaningful opportunity for specific skill or content instruction. A second grade teacher explained that she chose William Steig's *Amos and Boris* "to begin talking about descriptive words and how they are used to express a situation. Excellent to introduce synonyms." Similarly, another first grade teacher selected *Cache of Jewels* because "it is a content area book on collective nouns, e.g., cache, coven, kindle, swarm. It is literature that focuses on a skill, nouns taught in a meaningful context."

2. Personal/Aesthetic Factors

The selection of children's books for personal and aesthetic reasons was mentioned seventy-six times (45 percent). Sixty-three responses (37 percent) explained that the selected text was a personal favorite of teachers themselves or of their students. For example, a second grade teacher stated with reference to *Mrs. Frisby and the Rats of NIMH*, "I love this story and my students always do too. There are many important issues to discuss." A fourth grade teacher commented about Wilson Rawls, "I had read *Where the Red Fern Grows* and loved it, so I tried another."

Another seven responses (4 percent) indicated that they selected the book, in part, because it was an award winner (Newbery, etc.) or was considered a children's classic. An appreciation of the quality of illustrations was mentioned six times (4 percent) as a rationale for selecting the book. Characteristic of responses in this group were those of a first grade teacher who chose *Over in the Meadow* because it "had beautiful artwork" and of a second grade teacher who selected *Moses the Kitten* because "the illustrations by Peter Barret are heartwarming and delightful; I love cats and I always try to instill in my students a love for animals."

3. Gender, Race, and Ethnicity Factors

Only fifteen (9 percent) of the 170 responses suggested a recognition of the importance of considering gender, race, and ethnicity as factors in the book selection process. With regard to gender, seven teachers (4 percent) specifically identified it as a reason for selecting a particular book, some of whom reported a definite interest in the equitable presentation of males and females. For example, a fourth grade teacher selected *Danny, Champion of the World* because of its "positive male role model, strong single parent family, great adventure and coming of age novel for 9-12 years. The hero shows an inner strength of character that the reader can identify with." Similarly, she selected *The Wolves of Willoughby Chase* for its "positive female role model, dealing with loss of parents, home, and love, historical fiction with fast-paced action and adventure including villains who are outwitted by the courage of the heroine."

Several teachers expressly selected texts because the books connected an awareness of gender issues with particular classroom and social needs. For example, a fourth grade teacher found *Bridge to Terabithia* especially meaningful in portraying a sensitivity to social class differences and interpersonal relationships, "Having both a girl and boy main character helps ensure interest in this excellent book. The story emphasizes loyalty and imagination. A family with low economic income but high values is also featured. A lot of family feelings and togetherness is evident."

Other teachers commented on the importance of relating gender issues to the general curriculum. A fifth grade teacher describes *The Maude Reed Tale*, "This novel ties into our Middle Ages Unit. Its female protagonist struggles with what she is and isn't supposed to do, so it's a useful base for discussion of sex role stereotyping then and now. It contains a lot of information about the time period."

Similarly, a sixth grade teacher stated that she selected *Nobody's Family Is Going to Change* as "part of adolescent literature, taught in conjunction with our Human Growth and Change Unit. Deals imaginatively with puberty, self-esteem, overeating, sex roles, sibling rivalry, identity, and racism. Well-written, very appealing characters and plot, great for discussions, projects, and role plays." (This same teacher also indicated that this was only one of four children's books that she selected for this unit, the others being *A Day No Pigs Would Die, Summer of the Falcon*, and *Bridge to Terabithia*.)

Only eight (5 percent) of the 170 responses reflected a recognition of the importance of considering race or ethnicity in the book selection process. Many of these books represented historical rather than contemporary North American minorities. For example, a third grade teacher mentioned that she used *The Best Bad Thing* in her class because "the heroine's family is Japanese-American and second graders have studied Japan, the main character is similar in age to third graders. Writing is very humorous and forthright, but again the setting is a stretch: California, 1940s, heroine encounters prejudice, family struggles to survive, heroine is forced to reconsider an eccentric old woman with whom she is sent to live."

The Civil War was a catalyst for several of the book choices featuring Black Americans. A fifth grade teacher said of *Sounder*, "The main character is the age of my students. He is also a Negro child which helps the students to understand that race does not make us different as humans. The story takes place in the years following the Civil War and gives the students insight into the struggles of Black people in America." A similar line of reasoning was expressed by a fourth grade teacher who chose *Underground to Canada* "to give children a sense of what Black people endured during the period of slavery in the US. To stress the importance of freedom and treating people equally."

Books about Native Americans were most frequently historical accounts of the western expansion of Euro-Americans. A fifth grade teacher said of *Zeb*,

"This book deals with survival in the wilderness and relationships between European settlers and Native Americans, two themes central to our colonial Northampton [Massachusetts] social studies unit. It is at an appropriate reading level and students tend to enjoy it a lot."

A few teachers reported a commitment to selecting children's books relevant to the cultural backgrounds of their students. For example, a fourth grade teacher writes about *Call Me Bronk*, "This book mentions a concentration camp, displaced persons, and tells what it's like to come to a new country. The boy is from Poland. We live in a Polish community. It gives the students an idea of what the world was like when we were at war with Nazi Germany."

Finally, a sixth grade teacher in Massachusetts mentioned selecting *Spirit Ride the Whirlwind*, "Wonderful re-creation of Lowell, 1830, from the point of view of a 12-year-old girl struggling to help her family, move into a factory, to rise socially. Terrific precursor for a trip to Lowell and for developing themes, i.e., child labor, economics, social classes."

In reviewing the responses in each of these categories, we found that many teachers selected children's books as part of a complex, curricular process, focusing not on the book itself but on the context in which the choice made sense. Teachers frequently described a complex network of multiple, interactive factors which included, among other things, consideration of the children in their classrooms, their specific curricular needs, and the quality of the reading selections. Our study clearly reveals that, from many teachers' perspectives, the selection of a children's book generally was not a spontaneous, acritical decision made in an instructional vacuum. Rather, book choice was deeply embedded in the framework of a dynamic social setting (teachers' individual classrooms) and integrated into the context of larger curricular issues which included how to present a given unit of material in a thoughtful, meaningful way. More often than not, these decisions reflected approaches to instruction where the sometimes abstract and pedantic course content could be enlivened by the voices and pictures from children's books.

Conclusion

We think that two major conclusions can be drawn from the findings in this study. In the first place, the results of this study clearly provide empirical support for the existence of an "unconscious gender and racial bias in teachers' commonsense assumptions about 'what's appropriate for kids to read'" as identified in Luke, Cooke, and Luke's (1986) study of student teachers. That this bias is also characteristic of experienced elementary school teachers reflects the pervasive nature of the problem.

What does this mean for practicing teachers? It would be easy for us to suggest that teachers need to become more reflective in the book selection process, particularly to the implications of the selective tradition and the implicit exclusion, through children's book selections of the experiences of women and ethnic minorities. But how is this to be accomplished? Assuming that such teacher awareness might benefit from ongoing programs of professional development, an initial step might be to systematically arrange, as part of inservice teacher education programs, critical opportunities for exploration of the ideological aspects of teachers' book choice. For practicing elementary teachers, such opportunities could be presented in colloquia and/or workshops within a larger school- or district-based staff development course focusing on select issues in curriculum and instruction during a given school year. Such a professional education program has recently been developed in Maryland by the Montgomery County Public School system, a nationally recognized progressive school district located just north of Washington, D.C. For the past several years, MCPS teachers are required to participate in a three-credit, fifteen-session course (which is offered for graduate credit) entitled Ethnic Groups in American Society. Course sessions focus on a variety of topics which are designed to heighten teacher awareness of different American minority groups and to provide teachers with the skills and strategies for representing/including these groups' experiences across the curriculum. Perhaps as teachers are encouraged to consider the pluralistic nature of their school populations and to problematize their curricular decisions in staff development programs such as these, the inclusion of texts by and about women and ethnic minorities may assume more importance in elementary classrooms.

On a more individual basis, teachers can make use of a number of excellent resources to increase their understanding/awareness of the social and ideological implications of books they select for children. Some of the best are Robert Dixon's (1977) *Catching Them While They Are Young, Volume I; Sex, Race, and Class in Children's Literature*; the Council on Interracial Books for Children's (1976) *Human Values in Children's Books*; Leila Berg's (1977) *Reading and Loving* (especially chapters 20-25); and *Books Without Bias: Through Indian Eyes* edited by Beverley Slapin and Doris Seale (1988).

The second conclusion addresses the broader process of teachers' book choice itself and its implications for future research. The results of our study clearly reveal that teachers' selection of literature is a complicated, densely layered activity which involves a multiplicity of curricular, personal, aesthetic, social, and ideological factors, all of which vie for teacher attention in the contemporary classroom.

It seems to us that future investigation of teachers' selection of children's books for classroom use can profit from moving away from looking at each of these factors in isolation. Such decontextualized analysis, while providing important information, often flattens out the complicated landscape of book choice and smooths over the many curricular and conceptual issues that teachers struggle with when trying to decide how to incorporate literature in course material. We are currently exploring, for example, this more comprehensive picture of teachers' book choice by asking ten elementary teachers to keep a journal recording all the children's books they use in their classrooms during the entire school year and to write about why they have selected and how they have used them. It is our hope that such an in-depth study may more fully reveal the active dynamics of children's book selection, the degree of teachers' critical judgment, and which factors exert the strongest influence in both the definition and ongoing refinement of teachers' literary choice.

Commentary 2: Convention

The Selective Tradition in Teachers' Choice of Children's Literature: Does It Exist in the Elementary Classroom?

In this study, the first of our collaborative research projects, we took seriously the script for research production. We wrote, more than not, in the style to which we had been exposed, responsive to what we had learned to ask— reproducing what (we thought) was important for teachers to know. In retrospect, we now wonder if this is the language and essay structure our colleagues in the field prefer (or even choose?) to read. And we wonder how this project both bound and gagged our participants, taking them prisoner for our purposes. (In hindsight, it is not surprising to recognize that perhaps we also did the same to ourselves.)

The conventions of traditional research practice employed in this study now jar our identities as researchers. Who are we to condense and enumerate the experiences of classroom teachers? Who are we to shape and define their notions of being in the world? What (Who?) were we really searching for? Engaging in this form of research, we constructed a space of "otherness" within our inquiry, a designated homeland for the practicing teacher. Our language contains and defines their experiences, and our categories subvert their work as teachers to our progressive purposes. In doing this research, we inscribe their work in our time, in a particular history, in a particular social and cultural convention of our (p)reference and making. And we impose on them our intentions and a possible future, constituted as to what teachers ought to do— and why.

Again, in retrospect, it is easy for us to acknowledge that we did it all wrong. Central to our present understanding is that classroom research must not only be participatory in theory (as in: we propose, observe/interview/evaluate, analyze, write-up/ they cooperate— true non-participant observers of our research process), but must also be a research which supports an active, co-relationship, in both lived and represented form. Despite its analytic lapses and insensitivities to our colleagues in the field, however, the doing of this project has allowed us to discover the richness, and the importance of individual stories . . . it was the notes in the margins of the teachers' surveys, after all, that gave us the real "data" for understanding the process of teachers' book choice.

Now we have gotten out of the business of colonizing other teachers' experiences . . . although we fear we will never be able to avoid the colonization of others' ideas. We have reduced our subject pools, over time, from hundreds, to twenty something, to four or five, and finally now, to just ourselves. But we find ourselves still seeking the same stories, responsive to our own narratives, struggling to maintain the co-relationships and intersubjectivities that so eluded us in our early work. And the selective traditions we now study are our own.

Chapter Four

Inquiry

What questions are important? And which are irrelevant? (Irreverent?) How do we know? Which method helps us decide? And which leads elsewhere? When we disagree, what do we do? What do we say to each other? Do we try to work through these issues from an analytic base or an experiential one? Or is it primarily emotional? In struggling with these concerns, is our objective to achieve a unity? Are we happiest when our thinking develops along similar lines? Or are we confused? How long does it take us to get back "on track" if we don't think in the ways we expected? Can there be anything in thinking that is really "off track"? If it did matter once, how long did it take us to get over it? Is that why we never want to feel like that again? Can two people's thinking ever really develop along lines that are similar? Is that why two people decide to work together? To develop similarities? To say the same thing? To say the same thing twice? Or is this more difficult than it seems? If, for instance, one of us insists that the dynamics exerted on experience by time past are more central than those exerted by time present, what do we write about then? Or if one of us is interested in the unplanned and unpredictable fragments of daily life and the other is attracted by the fundamental role that privilege plays in personal and social development, how can we ever begin to write in a congruent way? Why do we keep trying to? Are we just forcing two into one to see how many times imagination can be reduced by methodology? Or are we creating a useful analytic tension? When does the useful become the contradictory? At what moment does the contradictory become the critical? When does it become useless? What force binds us together at the page level? Is it some unreasoning and ancient spell? Is it theory? What are the thoughts that surge just beneath the surface of our working lives? Our daily talk? Washing the car? Listening to an Orioles (or Packers) game on the radio? Choosing paint for the garage? Are these thoughts integral to our collaborations? To developing ways of knowing and methodology? To our commitment to both? To our commitment to each other? In what ways can we express how certain (zero?) events touch us? And how can we discuss their influence? Can we make ways never seen before, so that phenomena don't exactly fit into any premade analytic cubbyholes? Into "the box"? So that they come closer to life's sense of time, but don't reproduce the pseudo-histories of linear time? What falls by the interpretive wayside when we spend most of our time together thinking like this? What implication does this have for research? For standards? For standards-based knowledge? For discipline-based inquiry? What happens when one of us decides that the other just doesn't get it and speeds things up so there's an increase in the distance between us? How does this tension function? And what impact does it have on our collaborations? Does one of us sometimes secretly feel that we are running a race against the other in academic time? Do we bury this knowledge in our hearts and not talk about it? Is this something that's characteristic of other relationships, too? Does this make our commitment to each other stronger? Or weaker? What about the moments when we work independently of each other? When we work with other people? On other projects? Are we jealous of how the other allocates time? Are these allocations fair? Is anything ever fair? Or equal? Does it need to be? Who decides? If one of us likes to work on ten things with twenty people at once, is this just a different style of collaboration?

Is it a lack of commitment? To whom? Is this even an issue? What if one of our convictions is to leave things as raw and unfinished and rough-edged in our work and in our lives as we experience them? What is smooth or rough anyway? What does it mean to always revise, reorganize, rewrite, reconsider? When is enough enough? And in what ways do we make these surfaces, these competing interests in our work explicit as part of our work, too? Maybe even the major part? Is this too personal? Too nonstandard? Too contrary to the official rules and regulations of doing "real" collaboration? Is it worth taking the time to think this through? To talk this through? Is this one of those moments in interpretive time we should speed past in order to "make" time for something more important? Can we ever "make" time? If we decide to do something else, what kinds of things does our new surplus of time allow us to think about? What kind of name might we give this new space to distinguish it? "Explanatory not really explanatory?" Or "Method not quite?" Is this process of naming, of choosing a name, a creative act? Or a trap? Will its influence be felt? Will it transform anything? Do things exist only in the naming? Or do our questions establish just another kind of frame, a method, a kind of death, as Barthes (1975) once said? Do such processes transform thinking into a destiny? Work into an objective end? Disappear never to appear? Do we need to avoid this? How can we make ourselves write about what we really want to say in the ways we want to say it? When will we learn how to speak for ourselves? How will we learn to speak for ourselves? Can school help us do this? Can teachers help us learn this? If we transform the process of literal-conceptual, question-answer in order to understand things in a different way, what will happen? Will the old "base" cultures as David Byrne (1995) calls them, just fade away? Will the new imaginations make any difference? In interpretation? Or will they only become a new kind of culture that will end up looking like the old ones? Some of them already do, don't they? How do we peel back the multiple layers of ourselves as teachers and colleagues, readers and writers, and express some of these issues in a concrete way? In an effective way? In ways that create the kind of fracture zones in thinking that Foucault talked about so that we don't duplicate any more narratives? In ways that test the entire ideology of there being "a way"? A truth? An eternal light? Are these the real issues at stake in writing and teaching? In knowing and being today? In our collaborations? Or is this just our bias? And what about quotes: the specific thoughts of others? Why does one of us like to use them more than the other? Insecurity? Issues of ego and institutional power? Architectural support? How do words of others function in the real time of our work together? Do they add to the flow of our own thinking? Or do they act as substitutes for our own lack of words? Are they placebos? Are they shrines? To whose memory? Whose version of memory? Is it important to substantiate our ideas with those of others? When is this strategy documentation? When is it contextualization? When is it imitation? When is it adulation? When is it appropriation? When is it insemination? When is it theft? And when is it glamorous? When does it suggest real understanding? At what point does all the referencing get too contrived? Too derivative? Too far away from ourselves? Do we need a kind of fresh air on this particular issue? In what ways can we do this without creating another system? Are there really ever any new ideas under the sun? On some quiet afternoons or when we're shopping at the supermarket, how can we integrate the enjoyable imaginations that suddenly form in our minds into the center of our work? Like the simple (untitled) rapture that comes when we reflect on some parts of contemporary development? Dylan's new CD? Do these pleasures build up in layers inside us like the pyramids? Do they contain their own mysterious power like the tombs of old? Are there really any new ways of expressing the tensions between the excitements of the new and the very old ideas? Is enjoyment itself an issue in doing research together? Or is it only our concern? Should research be fun? What if most of the time we both just enjoy being in each other's company and talking with each other about music; the good stuff and the really bad stuff we've heard? Or about problems with relationships? Or about the over determinacy of astrological interpretations? Or how astrology is just another lens through which we focus interpretations? What if there are few direct economic or social benefits that can be drawn from these kinds of collaborative thoughts? And what about outcomes? What about competencies? What if few policy implications are the result of such work? What if little change occurs in classroom practice as a consequence of these questions? What if kids don't score higher on reading tests? What if they don't change their learning styles to reflect the richness and diversity of learning styles so necessary to have? For whom to have? What will Daddy say then? (How can we ever escape Daddy?) Does this kind of collaborative thinking really "work"? Is it even "real work"? Or is it a methodological (mythological) dodge? Is it a pedagogical problem? By which authority will we know? Or again: If one of us develops ideas in the interest of social justice and disrupting privilege and the other in the interest of a roaming artistic experience, are we two fundamentally different people? Do we need each other's different reality to help us construct a more vital, inclusive understanding of experience? If we keep asking these questions over and over and still over again in different ways, what does this suggest? That it's a condition for each of our identity's development? For knowing? For being? Or a contradiction? Is this the way things go: for us? Are we always teetering on the edge between the real and the abstract? How does gender influence the specific design of our thinking at any one time? Is there a perspective that is uniquely female? Uniquely male? Which is most real? And in what context? Or is this just another category from which to speak? (So to speak?) Is this a variable we're getting clearer about in our work, or is everything more mixed up? What is the consequence of trading roles? Of changing roles? Of blurring roles with the people you love? Of obliterating the kinds of structuralist and historicist interpretations that either deny or impose roles? That either deny or impose ways of thinking? Writing? Collaborating? Is this what Emerson once meant when he wrote about holding up a mirror and observing how knowledge develops in that blank space in front of us? Did one of us read that passage to the other once in earlier collaborative time? Or was it something else? Someone else? Was one of us not even there? Can we imagine a space when one of us is ever not there? Does knowing each other so well give us the power to write each other's words according to our own creative intuition and desire? Or forget them? Or finish each other's thoughts? Or steal each other's stories? Who said what to whom? Is this what we do as part of working together? Double-talk? Or is it talk doubling as a machine against forms of explanation and state-talk like Deleuze and Guattari (1987) want? Or seeds scattering in infertile/fertile ground? Whose words, ideas, passions finally reach these pages anyway? What happens to the specific "I" in the collaborative "We"? How many are there anyway? Who will know who the primary author is? Is anyone ever primary? Does it matter? Or is that, too, just another acquisition? Who is the first glamourizer, as Donmoyer (1991) puts it, of thought? Who will really know? Who will care whether the whole enterprise is just another blockade (machine?) against assuming the "collaborative"? What about the emotional consequences that collaboration and its double cause? What about the affective self? (Can one actually talk about such a construct without laughing?) What does this kind of wording tell us about ourselves and how needy we are? About the languages we've invented to specifically justify a few important things to exclude? Does this mean our emotions don't count in the work we do? What metaphors do the destructive forces of ego and competition assume? What happens when one of us begins the slow, aching spiral downward and thinks, Let's play the compare game? Who's getting the recognition? Who's getting all the press? When did we first learn how to ask: Who has more articles? Who has more ideas? Who has the more interesting ideas? Where did those crazy notions come from? Where did one of us read about the drama of two friends who like working together as they struggle to gain admittance to the upper class (theory???)? What if one of them starves? What if that, too, is just a perception? A justification? What happens to friendship as professional ambition, desire, and selectivity work their complex, brutal art? What does this fantasy represent? A projection? Is everything that is in the world, projected or otherwise, true? How can we know this? Do we mutually endorse this fantasy as an accurate depiction of (our?) outward lives? Or is this fantasy simply a singular invention unique to one of us? What happens when one of us violently (passively) disagrees? Will that fantasy be heard too? Or truth? How can one express these crazy, shifting, explosive emotions as a substantial part of what it means to be working and writing together? How can one unpack this potentially destructive power? Where does such an imagination (however fantastic) come from? Where can it go in writing about collaboration? And what understandings does it contribute toward getting a total view of the issue? How do we talk about this larger totality? And in what analytic form(s)? Will they be in and of themselves sufficient in enlarging our experience? Things change anyway, so what do we really have to lose? Do we have anything to lose? Was it almost three years ago (on New Year's Day in a telephone conversation from the beach at Lido Key to Santa Rosa), that we acknowledged that we pretty much worked together in this way? "Our work never starts with theory, but always with something else: is it love?" But love for what? Love for whom? And are we approaching that moment when we'll be missing the experience that we used to experience? When we'll miss the data (tears?) that we used to discuss? Miss the forms that defined our taste? Miss the parts about character and development? When we'll miss the opportunity to apply our generalizations to wider populations? When we'll miss the policy part when the wolf arrives at grandmother's house? Will the old ways once again become the new ways for us in the new America? Or does any idea work as long as we're talking about something we believe in, no matter how obscure the image, no matter how unusual the form, just as Neil Young says? What will these kinds of expressions mean for utopian thought? What will they mean for social practice? And the remaking of the social structure? What will happen to knowing and being? To research? What will become of these questions that we have such contradictory feelings about? And why not?

Commentary 3: Rejection

Inquiry

Sometimes we, too, wonder about the products of our imaginations. We originally submitted "Inquiry" for publication in somewhat different form and under the title "On Collaboration: Singular Reflections, Diverse Obsessions" in the National Council of Teachers of English journal, *English Education* where we had previously published several articles. This particular exploration emerged from our need to address the intellectual, personal, and emotional tensions that seemed to surge just beneath the surface of our collaborative efforts. We sought to confront the disruptions and contradictions we were feeling about our work and the direction it was taking, about working together, and the ambivalence we felt about making these tensions public. In retrospect, it was an attempt to make sense of the "underworld" of the collaborative research experience.

But exploring new worlds often requires new words (hooks, 1994, p. 167), so we tried to investigate these issues through an invented, alternative discourse that both evoked and spoke to the complex, swirling realities we were feeling. Ultimately, the editors of *English Education* decided not to publish "On Collaboration" in its submitted form, enclosing two reviews for our reference. The reviewers' comments concerned us— both because they cut directly to the heart of what, for us, constitutes collaborative research practice— the working through of issues of authority, identity, and emotion— and also because they each captured the fragility and tentativeness of our work together— our ever-self-renewing fear that our work might be seen as primarily narcissistic and meaningless endeavor.

For the purposes of this commentary, we have slightly modified and edited the reviewer comments for "On Collaboration" as shared with us by the editors of *English Education*.

Reviewers:

    1   &   2

To reject or not to reject?

Should we reject?   hosts of issues that constantly,

Will rejection hurt the rejected?   necessarily swirl around us

Is rejection bad?   acknowledge the human factors.

Is it good?   verbal and (for the moment) static

Was it seriously sent to me?   representation

Are you pulling my leg?   all those concerns & complexities

Is this a test?   perplexing, messy, fluid, exasperating

Sending this . . . to get reactions?   and inspiring concerns

Is there anything worth publishing?   in one place

Is this about collaboration?   issues are woven

Or about people infatuated with themselves?   (& re-woven)

And with each other?   a dazzling and sometimes

Was this written by college freshpeople?   intimidating tapestry

Who have a way with words?   and simultaneously taken

Who think their unoriginal ramblings   apart, even frayed

will find a place?   . . . too much to cover, too much going on

Someplace?   relentlessly entangling issues

Is this boring?   oddly familiar, like I had experienced it before

Self-congratulatory   my deeply-felt

crap?   but hard-to-express love

               of teaching.

Chapter Five

Fiction as Curricular Text

Any general review of the required reading lists of most teacher education courses in foundations, methods, issues, and curriculum reveals a fairly predictable array of academic, content-oriented texts. For many sensible reasons, including ready availability and the need to provide a "scientific" knowledge base, such materials have traditionally provided the basis for most teacher education students' reading and study programs.

A growing number of educators, however, aware of the value of such cognitively based reading selections yet sensitive to their limitations, are regularly assigning works of fiction as part of their course reading assignments. While the use of fiction as curricular text in teacher education courses may initially seem surprising, the idea has long enjoyed considerable support among many influential curriculum specialists and teacher educators.

As early as 1934, for example, John Dewey alluded to such practice. In *Art as Experience*, Dewey (1934/1952) noted that encounters with the literary arts enable individuals and teachers to cast off "the covers that hide the expressiveness of experienced things," thereby enabling us to "fin[d] ourselves in the delight of experiencing the world about us in its varied qualities and forms" (p. 104). Educators will recognize that this recommendation is, of course, in line with Dewey's repeated observations that all too often those "covers that hide the expressiveness of experienced things" are the ways knowledge is presented to students, abstracted in form and divorced from any meaningful connections to the experience of ordinary life. Encounters with literature and the arts, Dewey argued, clarify with special emphasis abstract material, condensing it into concrete form by focusing on the particular and the personal as they are reflected in the daily events, scenes, and complexities of human life. For Dewey, such kinds of experiential reference were fundamental to the development of fruitful programs of study for students at all levels. These advisements are also consonant with Dewey's wider efforts encouraging teachers to integrate subject matter across traditional curricular boundaries in order to promote more meaningful opportunities for student learning.

More recently, Maxine Greene (1978), Kieran Egan (1986, 1988), Diane Brunner (1990), and George Willis and William Schubert (1991) have similarly discussed the merits and potentialities of using such an approach with education students, associating encounters with the literary imagination with the development of a fuller attention to the lived world, a heightened perceptual fluency, and a discriminating consciousness, all of which, they submit, enlarge the capacity for effective teaching.

In our view, these well-reasoned linkages between literature and education are most useful. At one level, they contribute to the development of a theoretical framework for moving thinking about the preparation of teachers beyond an exclusive focus on instrumental/practical concerns to a broader understanding of determinants that might give such preparation more generous impress and form. This framework points to the generative power of narrative in educational discourse, if for no other reason than it makes problematic the long-held distinctions between the ideologies of what is "fact" and what is "fiction" in pedagogical practice. At a more personal level, such recommendations coincide with much of our own recent research in literature, curriculum, and teacher culture. A considerable part of this work has been a natural extension of our undergraduate programs of study in the humanities as well as our later graduate and professional interests in investigating the place of literature in teacher education. More specifically, for the past several years we have been collaboratively looking at teachers' use of literature in classroom settings, and the corresponding implications that such activity suggests for the development of curricular discourse and school knowledge (Paley, 1988; Jipson & Paley, 1991, 1992a).

Given this set of personal and theoretical interconnections linking literature to education, we found ourselves asking the following series of questions: What happens when contemporary teacher educators build on the impressive theoretical base articulated by Dewey and others and incorporate works of fiction into their courses? What issues guide book selection? How do they use them in class? What is the nature of student response to such unconventional instructional approaches? This article, the result of a study examining how contemporary teacher educators use literary works as part of their required course readings, provides some answers to these questions.

* * *

Six professors of education, including the authors, at three different universities (large and medium–size, public and private) participated in the study. Participants were identified on the basis of their experience using fiction as textual material in their courses, and all of them have been recognized as outstanding teachers by institutional award and/or by their colleagues and students. Case study methodology was used to capture the process of selecting and using fiction as curricular text. Course syllabi for each faculty member were examined, and course evaluations were reviewed when available. Participants provided, either in a twenty to thirty minute audio-taped interview or in a written statement, information about their reasoning, methodology, and recollection of student response to the use of fiction in their courses during a recent school year. Prior to the final draft of this article, participants had the opportunity to review their statements as situated within the context of a completed version of the article, and to make needed rewordings to insure statement clarity and fluency. The following section, highlighting portions of the responses of four participants, describes a complex landscape of opportunities for critical inquiry about issues germane to educators interested in the preparation of teachers for today's schools.

*   *   *

1. Professor X. teaches graduate courses in psychological development, social issues, and curriculum theory. Her discussion of why she found literature valuable in her teaching included the following statements:

> I try to connect the formal knowledge base for each of my courses with the personal experiences of my students. One way I can do this is by using literature, including poetry, drama, autobiography and fiction. My students, who are primarily female teachers and among whom are quite a large number of international and North American minority students, respond enthusiastically to non-traditional voices, those typically unheard in academic discourse. I use these materials to create an interwoven pattern of content and experience and to focus on the complex inter-relationships between faculty, students, text, and curriculum. Also these materials allow me to incorporate the perspectives of women and North American minorities into disciplines such as Developmental Psychology or Curriculum Theory where they are either absent from available textual materials or are represented in the objective, decontextualized manner of someone who has become the 'good academic.' In my classes

it's an issue of whose knowledge is reflected in the curriculum of my courses and how it is experienced. I want to include many forms of knowledge, multiple ways of knowing, and myriad voices so that my courses resonate with the complexity of people's lives.

She then talked about how this process actually "worked" in class, citing several examples:

I share with my curriculum classes from Virginia Woolf's (1938) *Three Guineas* where she talks about the educated woman who reads three daily papers and three weeklies, too. She reminds us that different texts vary about the facts and that to 'know' anything you must compare different versions and come to your own conclusions. We talk, in my seminar, about these multiple realities and the problematic nature of knowledge. I encourage their diverse theory making and interpretations, validating them as well as their ideas.

I also teach a class called Families and Schools and I use fiction to share alternative realities with my largely middle-class teacher-seminar students. Last term they chose from a list of contemporary fiction which I provided and which included texts that reflected a diverse cultural and gendered perspective. Students were asked to analyze images of the good mother, the strong father, and the competent child as we defined 'Family' and looked at family process. Barbara Kingsolver's (1988) *The Bean Trees*, Buchi Emechata's (1979) *The Joys of Motherhood*, Doris Lessing's (1988) *The Fifth Child*, and Tony Morrison's (1987) *Beloved* stand out as the stories that spoke most clearly to my students last term. Some said they had not taken the time to read a novel in years and were afraid to start, afraid, I suppose, of getting caught up in that more real world of the imagination where one must feel as well as understand. For many of the students, the novels presented an alternative to the ideal 'middle class' nuclear family they held as a model. It was particularly interesting as we talked about the 'family plot' idea from analytic psychology and how characters in very different novels and from very different cultural perspectives lived out similar dilemmas.

In addition to pointing out the problematic nature of "knowing," Professor X. also mentioned other reasons for using literary works in her courses:

> Sometimes I use fiction for very specific teaching purposes. In my Child Development class last term, I used short stories as part of an activity to clarify differences between major psychological theorists, including Piaget, Freud, Erikson, Skinner. Small groups of students were asked to analyze the experiences of children and adolescents in a short story according to a particular theoretical perspective. Then we compared what Freud, for instance, would say about a child's behavior to the explanation Piaget might give. In this case, fiction was used as an activity starter.
>
> I use quite a bit of poetry in my classes, too; deliberately, to engage attention, passion, and response. Susan Griffin (1982) [whose poem-play, 'Voices,' is used in class] talks about poetry as a way of knowing. She says that poetry gives to the political imagination a dimension of meaning without which it loses its way. She talks about the political nature of poetry and its ability to reintegrate mind and body, intellect and imagination. This makes a lot of sense to me and speaks to

my efforts to relieve the paralysis of what they call Cartesian anxiety, to step away from those horrible oppositions which define much of our academic discourse, and to renew our recognition of the multiplicity of human experience.

Finally, the language. I'm a former English teacher and I like to read aloud to my classes. We do a lot of listening to the way words carry meaning in their rhythm and sounds. I choose books, sometimes, because of the sound of the words and the poetry, like May Sarton's and Adrienne Rich's. Or because of the color of the book. I believe things like color, sound, story can transform the experiences of the reader; my students and I can help them invent a whole new world where text can be both an aesthetic symbol and a tool for a different understanding. The sounds and visions echo the meaning and amplify it.

2. Professor Y., who was recently honored as the outstanding teacher of the year at his university, teaches a three-course foundations sequence: Culture and Human Relations in Education and Society; Contemporary Issues: Culture, Curriculum, and Communication; and Multi-Cultural Curriculum. In each of these courses, he regularly assigns fiction in combination with traditional academic materials, films, and guest presentations "to give [his students] a broad-based perspective, to include the voices of cultural groups who are not represented or non-existent in the usual academic texts and courses." He said:

I want [them] to explore their personal and cultural values, behaviors, perceptions, and assumptions and I want them to map their primary cultural and cross-cultural awareness, development, and experiences. Through this process they can develop an awareness of, and identify, diverse cultural systems, potential points of conflict, and mediation or negotiation strategies that let them create teaching/learning experiences which address the full spectrum of human and cultural relations within their classrooms.

He then specifically discussed how this actually occurred in class:

In the first course, by reading and discussing books such as James Welch's (1980) *Fool's Crow*, Chinua Achebe's (1959) *Things Fall Apart*, Forrest Carter's (1986) *The Education of Little Tree* and Sandra Cisneros's (1985) *The House on Mango Street* in conjunction with Howard Zinn's (1980) *People's History of the U.S.A.*, Edward Hall's (1984) *The Dance of Life*, and the Sunday New York Times' Review of World News, students begin to look at history and current events from many perspectives and begin to see the interrelationship between them and cultural issues.

During one of the first sessions of the class we talk about the interactions between mainstream North American cultural values and assumptions and those of other cultures, addressing the question 'Is there a North American culture?' They've read Lisa Delpit's (1988) article, 'The Silenced Dialogue'; we [then] talk about whose experiences are part of the mainstream discourse.

During the second term we continue to explore personal and cultural interactions. We read both non-fiction and biographic literature [primarily written by and about women and North American minority cultures] and also excerpts from Jonathan Kozol's (1988) *Rachel and Her Children*.

We look at issues of culture and racism through people's experiences. For example, one guest speaker used material from Mary Belenky's *Women's Ways of Knowing* and *Rachel and Her Children* as well as her personal experiences with children in contemporary society. The class became very involved as they shared their own experiences as parents and children. They became very upset by the conditions Kozol talked about in his book. One class member, who works in a shelter, told her how they (the staff) were encouraged not to get involved with the families so they wouldn't become dependent. Then the discussion turned to nurturance and how the professionalization of teaching has made it difficult to be a caring teacher. We also talked about how caring is more acceptable in other cultural contexts. We also consider issues related to peace studies and environmental issues as we explore the inter-relationships between culture, community, and curriculum. Spring term we'll focus more on curriculum development and how teachers can integrate those perspectives into a relational curriculum.

Student response to Professor Y.'s approach has been enthusiastic. Written evaluations expressed a layered series of engagements, identifications, recognitions, and revelations of/with story characters and the dilemmas they encountered. Many students also commented on the patternings and rhythms of language and voice in the readings, expressing their surprise at how much these elements contributed to a deeper sense of understanding, command, and insight of/into course material.

3. Professor P. teaches undergraduate and graduate courses in educational foundations. For the past ten years he has taught Philosophical Foundations of Teaching and Learning. Required readings include selections from John Dewey, A. S. Neill, B. F. Skinner, Rousseau, and G. H. Bantock. Toward the end of the semester, students read a selection that many literary critics have long considered as one of the summits of Western literature: the section in Fyodor

Dostoyevsky's (1979 version) *The Brothers Karamazov* where Ivan Karamazov describes to his younger brother, Alyosha, his vision of human nature in The Grand Inquisitor. Professor P. reflected on his reasons for including such a reading selection in a course primarily concerned with issues of teaching and learning:

> I think the fact that I liked the text a lot. I found it very compelling when I first read it when I was sixteen years old, and I continue to find it compelling in the years thereafter. It speaks to so many different issues that interest me, so it's not very hard to weave it into teaching and writing. So many issues are richly depicted: the problem of evil, my own interests and questions having to do with freedom and authority, the capacity of human beings to be genuinely autonomous. [In Dostoyevsky's text] these issues lose their abstract quality; they acquire personality, acquire intensity, acquire a human face that makes them come alive to people who hear about them . . . these issues are implicit in story, [but] what's compelling is the story: The Inquisitor is locking Jesus up. What's going on here? We're drawn into the story, and issues that might seem remote [become very immediate] through story.

Professor P. then discussed how he used The Grand Inquisitor in class:

> Students read it in conjunction with a series of readings that extol human freedom and autonomy. It functions to question the course. The course worked with competing interpretations of what it meant for a person to become autonomous. Dewey gave one interpretation. And other educators different ones. The Inquisitor challenged the

foundation of that debate and what is taken for granted in our culture, namely, that autonomy is an attainable and desirable state. B. F. Skinner does the same but from a different perspective. I find The Grand Inquisitor's perspective more compelling. It speaks to issues I worry about that are intimately connected with education, such as the possibility of autonomy and the place of limits and guidance in education. It is a wonderful device for triggering thinking about these issues.

Another part is a not so hidden agenda to just get [my students] to read a great piece of literature and realize that good literature speaks to fundamental questions concerning our situation in the world.

When asked how his students have responded to his use of The Grand Inquisitor, Professor P. replied:

Very positive. Students generally enjoy reading the text and often get very excited about it. Not always, though: once, a student stopped me in the midst of some introductory remarks and complained that this was an anti-religious diatribe. Another student once complained that books dealing with religion have no place in a public university. Generally speaking, though, this selection from *The Brothers Karamazov* seems to make an important existential issue come alive for my students.

Professor P. then concluded his remarks by reflecting on other literary materials he has incorporated into his course:

Yes, I still use The Grand Inquisitor, but I use some different literary works as well, for example, William Blake's poem "The Schoolboy," Langston Hughes's "Ballad of the Landlord." I've been wanting to use *Huckleberry Finn* to get at a variety of issues that are germane to the work of educators— issues that concern the legitimacy of different dialects, and non-standard forms of English, dialect, issues of growth and development, as well as issues concerning the relationship, or lack thereof, between schooling and education. Was Huck better off growing up outside of school? Did his out-of-school experiences provide him with a superior education? There are also questions concerning racism and censorship triggered by Twain's description of Jim and his use of the word 'nigger.'

4. Professor Q. teaches undergraduate and graduate courses in teacher education. For the past fifteen years he has been incorporating works of fiction into his methods, foundations, and curriculum courses. For this study, he discussed why and how he used fiction in the course, Social Issues in Education:

In this course we explore a number of issues in contemporary American education and how they relate to the changing social order: the question of inequity in school and community, the dilemma of welfare, the debate over federal assistance to education, the controversy over what shall the schools of tomorrow teach in an increasingly pluralistic democracy, and so on. We also explore the issue of phantom students who have turned their backs to formal education. Students read Virginia Hamilton's (1971) *The Planet of Junior Brown* during this part of the course. *The Planet* is a young adult novel about two African-American boys, Junior Brown and Buddy Clark; both are in their early teens and both are growing up in New York City, alienated from mainstream culture. I use it for a variety of reasons. In the first place, it brings into our class, the voices and images of individuals who exist at the very margins of society and whose existence is conspicuously absent from most content-based texts. As we begin to focus our attention on their lives, numerous issues emerge from our reading: minority/majority relations, youth/adult interaction, the question of whether Buddy and Junior's intellectual and personal development is enriched or effaced by formal educational settings.

Student reactions to the use of Hamilton's book to get at these considerations have been, on balance, enthusiastic:

> Most students have tended to like the text quite a bit and when we discuss it their response is lively and energetic, but often unpredictable. Last semester, for example, one student raised an important issue. She insisted that this book shouldn't be read by children, or by preservice teachers either, precisely because it was so strange and unsettling. She referred to the total craziness that permeated the boys' shadowed lives in New York; Buddy's planets of homeless children living in the ruins of abandoned buildings in Manhattan, and Junior's unbalanced, dominating mother and crazy piano teacher. Why does anyone need to read about this distorted way of life? Her deeply felt remarks prompted other students to defend the book. A discussion about the kinds of literature suitable for children followed, which then led the class into a consideration of censorship. This wasn't what I had planned, but it suggests the level of engagement this class

experienced with the book.

I also like to use *The Planet* because it's so artfully crafted. I want my students to encounter powerful literature and enjoy its complex aesthetic satisfactions and tensions beyond the academic level. I want them to see how a piece of writing can dazzle you like a beautiful jewel can dazzle: I mean, if you really look into it and if you look carefully, you're confronted with a stunning series of internal reflections and counter reflections and you say: 'What is this?' I want my students to be stupefied that this kind of beauty can happen at any moment, even in a course concerned with issues in teacher education.

Finally, I use it because of my own educational background. My undergraduate minor was French Literature and one of the clearest memories I have about it was when we read Camus, and the difference I felt in his writing about existentialism in his novels and then again in his more formal works like *The Rebel* or the *Lyrical and Critical Essays*. I don't recall anything, really, from *The Rebel* or the *Essays*, but I do remember *The Stranger* and the hero, Meursault. In fact, even today I can remember the very first sentence of the book, you know: 'Mama died yesterday or maybe it was last week . . .' or something like that. I also remember Camus' description of the blinding summer sun of Algeria and how when Meursault shot someone he did not know on the beach on one of those blinding days, Camus very carefully wrote: 'and the trigger gave way.' So did Meursault really mean to shoot him, I wondered? Was he really guilty after all? How can we be certain? To what extent is this elusiveness in Camus' story characteristic of things I experience in my life? The point of all this is that, for me, 'existentialism' became a much more vivid, and memorable, experience in Camus' fiction than in his philosophic investigations. It's been more than twenty-five years since I first read *The Stranger*, and Meursault seems to have taken up permanent residence in my life. The same with Stendahl's Julien Sorel, or Dostoyevsky's Ivan Karamazov and Raskolnikov and Prince Myshkin. Or Jack Burden from *All the King's Men* and [Doris Lessing's] *Martha Quest*. Robert Coles (1989) talks about this persistent, powerful, invasive quality of literature in his recent book, *The Call of Stories*. I want my students to sense the power of these invasions too, and perhaps as a consequence, to be able to communicate it at some future point to their students when they become teachers.

Professor Q. concluded with these reflections:

Recently, I've been thinking about using Flannery O'Connor's short story, 'Everything That Rises Must Converge,' as a kind of final reading in the last course [Seminar in Student Teaching] that our students are required to take before they start looking for teaching positions. Her way of placing the entire intellectual enterprise in jeopardy. She says something important to all of us, I think, in this story, but her observations seem especially pertinent for teachers. Yes, the knowledge-base is important. Yes, content must be mastered. But I'm convinced that Thomas Merton was on to something when he suggested somewhere in his writings that knowledge wasn't necessarily the greatest attribute of a 'learned' person, nor was it the most important part of intellect. There's the whole issue of humility too. To teach with clarity, of course, but also with a fundamental sense of charity. I've always felt that this quality needed to be addressed and I've never really come across it in any required books in education courses. Maybe Herbert Kohl's *36 Children*. Anyway, it would be interesting to see how our students might respond to O'Connor's devastating insights into human pride and individuals' use, and abuse, of knowledge.

* * *

While each of these educators has selected different works of fiction for use in a wide array of education courses and while their choices seem deeply embedded in a complex framework of individually determined curricular and pedagogical factors, we think that there are several themes common to all that merit attention and brief discussion.

The first is the use of fiction to ensure the representation of a diverse cultural perspective in course material. The experiences of women, people of color, and certain social classes are particularly highlighted. This suggests that the professors we interviewed were aware of the recent criticism by a diverse group of educational sociologists, curriculum specialists, and literary theorists who have pointed out that the representation of such voices is too often excluded from the curriculum in favor of books featuring predominately white, Anglo-European, male authors and subjects. The professors we interviewed also seemed alert to the fact that such exclusion has pedagogical consequences; that is, it diminishes the legitimacy of one group in favor of another and presents students with an ideologically biased, culturally exclusive, and ultimately false view of society. By incorporating works of literature by and about groups whose existence is traditionally depicted as marginal to mainstream society, these professors present their students with a more accurate, more complex, perhaps more problematic view of education and school knowledge. As one instructor remarked: "[I]t's an issue of whose knowledge is reflected in the curriculum of my courses and how it is experienced. I want to include many forms of knowledge, multiple ways of knowing, and myriad voices so that my courses resonate with the complexity of people's lives."

The second common theme that clearly emerges from our interviews is professors' use of fiction to make concrete in the minds of their students the course material that is too frequently abstracted from any meaningful human experience. Several professors specifically described how issues of authority, autonomy, minority majority relations lose their abstract qualities when expressed in fiction; or, as one professor positively cast it: "they acquire personality, acquire intensity, acquire a human face that makes them come alive to people who hear about them." While the practice of firmly connecting abstract principles to experiences in everyday life is hardly a revolutionary concept, it bears repeating since so much conventional educational activity continues to encourage the study of an impersonal, ahistorical body of material that is divorced from the interests and lives of students. Again, reference to Dewey is instructive on this point. Referring in *Art as Experience* to the educational power of literature, Dewey observes:

> Words as media are not exhausted in their power to convey possibility. Nouns, verbs, adjectives express generalized conditions— that is to say *character*. Even a proper name can but denote character in its limitations to an individual exemplification. Words attempt to convey the *nature* of things and events . . . That they can convey character, nature, not in abstract conceptual form, but as exhibited and operating in individuals is made evident in the novel and drama, whose business it is to exploit this particular function of language. For characters are presented in situations that evoke their natures, giving particularity of existence to the generality of potentiality. At the same time situations are defined and made

concrete . . . Ethical treatises in the past have been impotent
in comparison [with literature] in portraying characters so that
they remain in the consciousness of mankind. (Dewey
1934/52, p. 243)

When abstract material is connected to the vicissitudes of daily life through
fictional structures and characterization, its intensity seems to have an existence
that is remarkably enduring. Long after the course is completed and forgotten,
story characters, and the "situations that evoke their natures," continue to live.
Conversely, abstractions seem to have an impermanent, unstable life span; one
professor's recollection of his undergraduate readings in existentialism by
Albert Camus is a case in point.

Finally, several of these instructors deliberately incorporate literature into
required course readings for its artistic value. Two features are important to
note about this theme. First, the faculty members we interviewed all expressed
a lively sense of what it means to be well-read beyond one's own academic
specialty, and they exhibited a commitment to encouraging the development of
similar values in their students. They considered encounters with literary works
and with their constitutive elements such as the rhythms of language, the
intricate layerings of meaning, the artful reconfiguration of the human
condition in ways so new that their appearance is often startling, valuable for
future teachers to experience and enjoy, not merely in isolation in English
courses, but as a fully integrated component of students' professional study in
education.

But there is more than just this. The responses also allude to a deeper, more
complicated value than encountering literature for mere aesthetic pleasures. As
several of these instructors suggest, and as George Steiner (1989) more
explicitly points out, literature and its address to the reader, is totally direct and
overwhelming in its indiscretion (pp. 142–143). If it is good, if it is authentic,
literature unremittingly asks us the most penetrating questions. What do you
think of the possibilities of this life? What do you feel about the alternatives to

existence which are implicit in your experience of me, in our encounter? How will you arrange your life now?

These persistent interrogations, and the complications they provoke in the very center of our being, are rarely formalized with such intrusiveness, such immediacy in content-based texts. When incorporated in students' professional education programs, their pertinence may well awaken future teachers to a much more powerful, complex image of what teaching is, and what it also surely can be.

Commentary 4: Hiding

Fiction as Curricular Text

For some time, we have been thinking about the notion of research as fictional text. Constructing our own subterfuge, burying our own understandings in our interpretations of others' experience, we have often, during our collaborative work, wondered about the ethics of consciously creating our own invisibility in the research process. Not that we ever thought we could not be detected— but often, under the guise of impartiality and (shudder) objectivity, we found ourselves concealing our presence, hiding out from our readers, creating a cover-up, a work of real fiction— at least on the surface of things. In retrospect, we have come to recognize that by secreting ourselves in the research process, we actually were creating a kind of "object permanence"— revealing a previously unconstituted identity, an alias (and an alienation?) to the very experiences we chose to analyze.

It was doing the research for "Fiction as Curricular Text" that we began to realize our own complicity in the mystifications of research. We had conducted this study as one of the initial moves in our own struggle to escape from "the tyranny of statistics, control groups, tight treatment design, contrived variables, compulsive measurement, meaningless surveys" (Wolcott, 1994, p. 414) into the seemingly safe haven of narrative. We had little awareness at the time of the equally complex issues involved in doing interpretive research.

For this study, we chose to interview academic colleagues about how they used fiction as curricular texts in their college and university courses. We don't remember if it was because we were short the number of informants that we needed, or if it was because we thought our own stories were at least as rich as those being told to us by our colleagues, but when we came to choosing the narratives for inclusion in our paper, we somehow came to the decision to "interview" each other and to use our own stories, too. Not totally comfortable with our decision to situate ourselves as participants in our own study, and perhaps fearing collegial critique in those early days of narrative and postmodern research in education, we "hid" our identities and blended our stories in with all the others. Carefully creating an artifice, we distanced ourselves from our own deeply held belief about the teaching and learning experience: to make identity's power more visible in the curriculum, and to create opportunities for our students to engage with such realities in an up-front way. Later, influenced by the autobiographical honesty of researchers such as Harry Wolcott (1990), Madeleine Grumet (1988), and Janet Miller (1990), we began to rethink our decision.

Considering Diamond, Arnold, and Wearring's question (in Diamond & Mullen, 1999, p. 427), "How can researchers show they are part of the research story they tell?", we now recognize that we were "hiding out" in our research. And yet, perhaps this very process of "hiding" provoked useful tensions— tensions which we could no longer support or maintain, and pushed us to eventually confront the fictionalizations we were making. And we have begun to uncover a new kind of visibility— a research writing that is so transparent that the distinctions between researcher/researched are made obscure and all positionings turned back upon themselves, so that— as Diamond, Arnold, and Wearring suggest, "all participants are located on the same reflective surface of inquiry" (in Diamond & Mullen, 1999, p. 429).

Chapter Six

Fantasy

1

She touched his arm, and without looking up, he immediately knew it was time. He arose and began to smooth the covers back in place, absently feeling the delicate weave of the fabric rustle and separate at his fingertips, a hundred small blossoms of pleasure absorbed by his touch. Tonight, she would be the one to begin everything. She would be the one to select what would happen at that indispensable location they now returned to again and again in their minds. Years of practice turned into night. Turned into burn or pleasure in his mind. He looked straight ahead, toward her, without intent or suspicion, just as they had learned. Making the first move, she felt herself step forward out of herself and then into herself, and out of and into time. Somewhere— so far away now —what might have been thunder rolled over the house. Then a long moment of silence, and then the deeper silence in which they turned toward each other like that first moment so many years ago. Still startled by how everything could always be so new, she felt a delicate blaze whisper on her skin: a little, flickery rapture. Once again, there was always so much to know. There was always so much to reach out for.

2

It wasn't always like this, although it was difficult to remember how, over the years, they became the familiar routines that named them now. During their initial encounters, change was what they were, and what they saw in each other seemed like their own longing for what was always new. This fascination, and how it grew into something they disappeared into (a series of reflections after vanishing reflections), would take them years to recall. But in that original time, there were as many mysteries as necessities. And, from the beginning, she was more open about hers. Driven by her intense imagination (or was it the desperation that was chasing her?), she had made it clear that there were other dimensions to who she was, other places to which she always needed to belong. (At that time he read them as Runaway.) Much later, when nothing she did really startled him anymore (Was he wrong about this, too?), he saw how so many other names would rise in her mind to be formed into herself, in order to be changed by herself, like almost everyone else. But he did not let himself believe that this would be his own ending, too.

3

Hesitating, she turned the brass key and slowly stepped aside as the heavy door swung open. The room was as she remembered it from so long ago, in that time when she still believed he would come for her. She looked around, noticed the heavy moss-rose draperies, now drawn haphazardly to a partial close, yet not quite concealing the high window and the faint shadows of the pine trees brushing up against the glass. Shuddering in the damp closeness which enveloped the room, she glanced about again. The wardrobe, still filled, no doubt, with her gowns, was to her right. Before her, the dark mahogany table glowed in the reflected light of the candle stub perched on its surface. She moved toward it. Yes, the letter was still there— lying in the box where she had placed it the last time. "Go to the country house and wait, I will come for you."

How many years had it been? How many times had she reread that letter, certain that he would appear in that moment and take her away to the special place they had created for their escape. She slipped it back into the envelope. She could not afford this dream now. She needed time to think. But that would come later, after she had prepared herself.

She busied herself, readying her bath. The steam rising momentarily from the cold marble of the tub reminded her of the hopelessness of her plight. It was all an illusion—and in a moment it, too, would all be gone and the cold loneliness would return. As she trailed her hand across the still surface of the water, spreading the lavender blossoms about, she once more rehearsed the question—what am I to do? And then, her robe slipping from her shoulders, she stepped into the bath, extending her legs the length of the enclosure and resting her head against the welcoming softness of the towel she had placed on the ledge.

What to do? To pretend, again, that it had not happened? That he would come, this time, for good? To believe the letter after all, after all this time? But that would be a mistake, she knew, a perhaps fatal error. And yet, she yearned to escape, to exit this perplexing maze in which she always found herself, to return to the simplicity, the elusive security, that she remembered as her past— to the place where things had seemed to happen just one at a time. But such dreaming went nowhere. What could she do now?

4

From the beginning, she seemed convinced about their being together, about their destiny. So it wasn't surprising that it wasn't he who chose her, but rather it was she who selected, from the surplus of available events and time, possibilities and life situations which were available to her at that moment, his own particular tempo, his reality. But, as they were to find out later, promise was one thing and consequence another. As they began working together, a part of him would marvel at how very close she would often come to him in order to make him disappear into what she wanted them to both be, and he marveled at the immense enjoyments that this kind of interaction seemed to provide her: the hidden romance that's always wanted, but that never exists except in adventure stories that don't last. It was as much from this form as another that their involvement evolved, and he often felt himself thinking how easy it would be for anyone, given similar circumstances, to maybe fall into the same kind of place. Eventually, he learned that pleasure, for her, was whomever she could find in time, but he also began to see how this need was connected to no one real because of her own fear of someone real. So sometimes late at night, after they'd finished trying out one more new routine and as both of them were just about to be overwhelmed by sleep, he thought he could hear her dreaming about how all she ever wanted was to be loved (was to stop the aching); and, wide-awake now, he could literally see her moving toward and away from visibility, as if looking for the person that she kept pretending was someone else.

5

In those days, they did almost everything together. In retrospect, they could not recall when they began to let these interactions replace daily life, and how more and more of the moments they spent together replaced ordinary time. And so, much like most everyone else, the experiences to which they contributed became the moments they most desired; and these circumstances soon began to identify them for who they were. Eventually, the hours they spent together transformed each of them; and in the dense, emotional spaces of this accumulated time, it became more difficult to identify who would be the originator and who the distributor of the other's ideas. It was in some of these ways that they found each other sometimes speaking simultaneously, sometimes saying what the other almost thought. Once, he told her that he imagined their discussions resembled the sounds made by falling leaves. Another time, he remembered how she had warned him about continuing to make those kinds of associations, since that kind of thinking always transformed experience into something it never really was. But because of his own insecurity about what he believed in, he took what she said and let it go at that.

6

She hadn't intended to be unfair, after all, or to betray that special bond that seemed to exist between them for all time. It had begun so innocently— in her vulnerability she had not expected the events to roll together so rapidly and in just that way. She was as surprised as he. And yet, looking back, it had seemed inevitable— as if they had been awaiting that moment their entire lives. She knew that she owed him, at the least, her honesty. And perhaps, more importantly for her own survival, she owed herself that same kind of honest regard. But now, to let go. To admit that he was not going to come, not in the way she wanted, was never going to be there in the way he had seemed to promise.

"I hope I've not deceived you, led you to expect more than I can be . . . it's just that . . ." She recalled how his words had trailed off and how she had once again assured him that it was all right, that she expected nothing more from him than those brief moments, those strangely absent embraces. And somehow, somewhere inside, she recognized that she could never be with him for more than the moment, for more than the moment of his need, that it would never work for them, either. But that, of course was the source of her present turmoil, the reason why she had returned here one last time. Just what was real? Even now she was unsure. Even now she still hoped for his arrival.

7

Long before they learned about each other's specific needs and long before they developed what later became their fantastic routine, he recalled how she used to play The Story Game. In those early years, they had comparatively little experience with each other to draw on, so their obsessions emerged naturally, as they interacted with each other in the visible world. But as more and more of their workdays turned into evenings together, he saw how she would increasingly need to disappear into a deep part of herself; and it was during these moments of disappearance that she would momentarily forget where she was and begin to talk about what had happened to her when she was a young girl. At first, her frankness startled him (since it clashed with his own indirectness), but eventually this, too, became a part of their routines and as familiar as any other. The basic themes of The Story Game were always the same. There was the story about her grandmother, who held her tightly in order to help her grow up. There was the story of her mother, who taught school in order to die young. There was the story of her father, who disappeared in a war and never came back alive in the same life. There was the story about the hen's neck on the stump and the moment of sacrifice which she could never forget. There was the story of her recurring dream of how all she ever hoped for was a small cottage of her own with cozy rooms and windows that looked onto a flowering garden where she imagined herself picking blackberries or enjoying tea. There was the story of the spiral sea that she invented for herself alone. During these moments when she played the Story Game, her own voice fell away, and the desperation in her words fell away, and the magma that she felt within her and within her world fell away, too. In the beginning, he didn't know what these stories meant, but he trained himself to follow her voice as it narrated, always following a familiar path, always using the same words, always repeating the same images, what she carefully respected as valuable in order to later throw away.

8

It had all begun innocently enough, a simple lunch, old friends, wine, talk. The walk along the beach had been, in its own way, a warning. She could still almost feel the warm sand on her neck, the damp wind against her face. He had embraced her, to keep her warm, he said. They had talked, relived old memories, spoken of what they had once been for each other, comforted each other against their separate losses, their mutual loss of each other. The idea had not occurred to them fully-formed but rather had slid into their conversation so silently that it seemed as if it had always been there. They could go on, again. And why not? It was the most natural thing— and away from everything familiar, it happened.

Of course it would happen. That was the way it always was with them— the one thing they could always count on. And for a while it seemed to work, expanding their worlds with its promise. Across the long absences, the letters and calls maintained the elusive and fleeting fiction of their closeness. Once he flew out to the coast and they drove along the ocean again, together. Another time, they sat by the stony shore and watched the few boats struggling against the current. She knew it was dangerous. She knew that when he had gotten what he needed from her he would again leave and she sensed that what he wanted was really not her, but the confirmation, the continuity that being with her provided. But for her to truly acknowledge this, to name the power he held over her was impossible. Because what could she do then? There was no other way. Instead, she thought, she always chose to, was forced to, bury thoughts of all other possibilities. All other explanations. Only one thing at a time, certainly no one could fault her for that. Fleeting visits, lunch, the lack more apparent than the presence, but a faint promise, none-the-less. And later, always, betrayal.

9

He was fascinated by the sensations she evoked in him, and by their variable nature. A drive along the California coast together one stormy afternoon in late November produced in his mind as glorious a sense of thanksgiving as ever in his life existed. Another time, deep in the interior of an insoluble tension between them, he watched, with the clearness that only indifference brings, how he was already drifting away from her even as he watched each of her lifeless explanations flutter to the ground. At that moment in that time, he felt the splendid sensation that he had absolutely no interest in ever seeing her again. Another time, he felt numbed by the consequence of yet another broken promise and missed engagement and choice she made, cleverly dividing him in her divided mind, in order to be whole, herself, and elsewhere. During these moments, he learned how it was completely understandable that one day his feeling for her would no longer be any real concern of his, and that this was a sensation he could feel vibrating throughout his whole being. And then, more times than he could count, he felt how he was also flooded with such unbearable tenderness for her as he suddenly heard her say how lonely she really was. If these sensations didn't add up to much, they at least provided a different context in which they could reflect, amidst all the diagonals and divisions, about what really counted in the process of their connected labors, and why.

10

The ways that she relentlessly devoured style after style, and person after person, in place after place in the dizzying number of locations she inhabited both amazed and startled him. From what motivation did this devotion come, and what form would be its consummation? "Teach me," she once whispered to him in an embrace so astonishing that he could not honestly say if it was yet another one of her own imaginations, "teach me to care." But what could he possibly say to her that she did not already know? This incoherent world? This sometimes lovely life? The places she left, burned behind her ("Teach me not to care?") and the more she searched for meaning, or for an interpretation never before seen that might provide a different costume for her newest identity, the more these things seemed to elude her. Eventually, she became her own dispersal. She became the many faces she was. During these moments, when the speed of the process appeared impossible to maintain still one more time in yet one more place, she would return to the only thing that gave her what she wanted. Then, night after night, she would be ready to resume their incredible routine, awakening after having cried herself to sleep about her own fragmentation, refreshed by the hope that this private act of destruction (through its own fragmentation) might become a stage for something redemptive, something sacred. Then, in this new perfection, she would reach out to him, and he would feel all over again the absence dancing inside of him like some lonely star, so near to this world.

11

No one expected them to exist like this, and no one cared if they did. But this made them feel free, and sometimes that feeling was as overwhelming as any faraway promise. Every new experience seemed to throw them away from each other and toward each other in new, unidentified space. As they repeatedly struggled to acculturate themselves to whatever new surroundings they found themselves in, they wrestled with the uncertainties of how useless most of their prior experience was and how irrelevant many of their behaviors were. During this time, they still weren't concerned that they weren't becoming anything yet, so they weren't really trying to find some external point that they could use to interpret their attachments to all the things and events they experienced together. All of this was not as easy as it sounded, nor was it entirely successful. Having no systematic plans for the life they were living, one choice led them to another. Still, from this lack of structure, a kind of structuring process emerged; and as they began to experiment with different routines and different ways of knowing each other, they found themselves believing in some mystic inevitability. It was primarily in these alternative kinds of spaces that both of them came to create the practices that they eventually would be using, and which would eventually use them.

12

She remembered that first time, how she had not anticipated his rage or the sullen voice that accused, cut so close to her soul. She had dared suggest something more. His response was sudden and cruel. No expectations . . . as if her whole life did not depend on the expectations that he offered. What could her life possible be without the promise of more?

Enough. The water had grown quite cold. Shivering, again, she stepped out of her bath, wrapping the heavy quilted robe about her body. "This must end," she thought, "now."

Resolved, and, as always, firm at those moments when she had chosen to remember the painful parts, she re-entered the main room. She knew what needed to be done. Opening the small drawer at the center of the desk, she placed the letter carefully at the bottom, sliding the blotter over it, wedging it between the small fabric box and the photo of that autumn day on the beach.

13

In the videos that he knew she was making of herself (and of their own parallel conversations), he imagined her creating narratives that were not even remotely subject to the usual protocols of narrative. Character, relevance, and application were only existing footage from which she spliced together whatever she needed to make, for whatever she wanted, for whoever would listen. The result would be a new kind of story: edgy, suggestive, inconsistent. After all, wasn't it she who had introduced him to the resources of negative possibility? As he imagined her with her camera, he saw her struggling to examine her own impulsiveness and desire (those impulses toward wholeness that she desired?). Once, in a different context, when she told him how she truly believed that all her loves would be always hopelessly lost, he remembered the overpowering sense of incompleteness that he felt for why things could be as they were. He imagined her trying to represent the hugeness of all this and wondered whether or not it would matter to anyone if she did. How was it possible to represent the mysterious in life, just when what was mysterious seemed to be routinely transformed into something impossible? Sometimes the enormity of this paradox confounded them, and they sensed it was more than they could hope to decipher. It was in this complicated way that he loved her; that he felt closest to her— as when some people find themselves doing the right thing in the wrong way.

14

And now to prepare, she thought. Will it be the violet silk? The black? Her hands rested on the soft brocade, the color of the sky just as the sun disappears below the horizon of the sea. She must make everything right again, the way he would want it. She would begin again. There was no other way. She walked to the table where a single, small object remained. Perhaps a talisman. He had given it to her after all. Carefully sweeping it into her pocket, she fondled it, then folded her handkerchief over it, a fringe of the white lace trailing out the side. And opening, again, the door, she heard herself say, "I am ready."

For the first time, perhaps, she was truly afraid. What was it he really wanted from her? This coming and going, the incessant plea, his deep-pitched voice again and again and again, reminding her of before. And then there were his movements, the very way his body leaned toward her as they passed on the stair, all suggesting at that same desire, expectation, unnamed, perhaps unimagined by either of them. No. She could not let this happen again.

15

Once, but long before they had developed into what they became, he had given her one of his small paintings in gratitude for the kindness she had shown him at a difficult moment in his life. If many things were made in this world, as he had once read somewhere, to help you forget yourself, he wanted to make something for her to help her remember herself. The painting he gave her was monochromatic and non-referential, with layers of paint scraped away so that whole areas were only partially covered. To give it structure, he had placed it within a narrow, white-painted wood frame he had made himself. To his eye, it could always be many things, but he especially liked how sometimes its densely scarred surface seemed to glow with a kind of light and dark— like fire, he thought— it was almost something that used to be one thing but is not yet the next. She hugged him upon receiving it, and then she hung it over her fireplace. The formalization of fire. As the years went by and as she kept devouring her own psychology as fast as she could invent it, he was touched that she always kept his painting, even as she tried to satisfy her need for fire by changing almost everything else.

16

The trip down the coast had been interminable. The driving rain against the window obliterating any attempt at real conversation. They had talked of small things, the rain, the wine they had shared at lunch, the triumphs of their respective children, the little disappointments of their work. But still unsaid were the real questions that had brought them together again, had brought them back to this place, again. What would happen? What would be done? Was either of them really ready to take the next step, to move on to the promise of something that might never really work, anyway? Perhaps it was too important to risk— to have this finally fail might devastate them both for all time. Perhaps it was the promises that counted most, after all.

Why was she so afraid? She trusted him, that was without question. Or at least, she had always thought she trusted him. But sometimes . . . she recognized now that sly, boy-smile that crossed his face whenever he was unsure. That apologetic, pleading look of hesitation, of uncertainty, about her, about what she would do, about what he wanted her to do. But that was not at all his fault, he couldn't be blamed for her indiscretions, her lapses, after all. Perhaps that was it— if only he could understand the intensity with which she desired certainty, her raw need caught up in those tired, once playful, gestures. Did she fear that he would not understand— or perhaps that he would? Stripped of the velvet, and the glistening words, would he see her for what she really was? For what she feared she might already have become? If only they could go back, back there where it always seemed to be all right, at least for the instant. But that had become more and more difficult. Too many others making their demands, exacting their contingencies. And it never lasted, either. When he had gotten what he wanted from her, he would always disappear again, until the next time.

17

Outside, the storm intensified, and a lashing rain beat against the windows of the house. It was at moments like this that everything seemed most calm. They would be enjoying each other's company at the harmonium and she would fold her hands into small faces and look directly into his eyes and begin to tell him her dream about the wolves. Both of them always pretended the wolves were something new. Usually, the dreams she retold to him had nothing to do with them at all; many of her dreams consisted of things: things misplaced which she had secreted away and then couldn't quite find, parentless objects that had escaped her ambition and then her recollection, no matter how earnestly she searched. The wolves were new. She told him that some of them came from the wolf skin that belonged to her father (so they functioned as an example of the living and the dead), or they came from an image of all that lies beyond the far mountains, or they were a whisper on the other side of sleep. Those kinds of wolves. There were also, of course, the others. Some, she said, belonged to her grandmother, who once, when she was young in the apple wood grove, came upon a real wolf walking toward her in the certainty of his belief. She met him on the path of fortune and, in a sudden reversal of roles, heard herself say that it was she, the surprising self, the self tired of living the same way and telling the same story— and so, without waiting for him to howl for mercy, she separated him from their terrible dream with her ax. But then there were the wolves who survived all self, and all surprise. They looked directly into her heart (following her beloved Rilke?). These were the wolves she feared the most, and her fear was reflected in the mirrors of their eyes. Quick and unstable, they reminded her of things that were never quite there, so she couldn't tell if they were attempting to communicate anything to her or just incapable of doing so. In these moments, she felt herself become at least two things at once, and it was at this point that she would either stop, because there was nothing else she could say; or she would go on, because there was nothing else she could do.

18

He extended his hand, smiled, stepped close. Head tilted to the side in that always-engaging gesture of affection, he indicated his approval. In anticipation of his request, she moved aside, turning as if to acknowledge the ever-present reality of her shadow. Then, taking up her hand from where it lay in her lap, he motioned, "Come now." She followed, the long dark hall engulfing her in its shadows. They would begin again and then, most likely, again and then again. What else was there? The other, unthinkable. That chance was over, abandoned, it had been this way for far too long.

But for now, the betrayal was set aside. The occasion was all too apparent, seductive, even, in its rich possibility— there was no other option, really. And once it started it would all come easily— she knew that. It always did. But the choice? Where was the choice? And was it worthwhile without it? Could all the adulation given her ever compensate for those missed opportunities? For the hints of scorn? For all those years waiting? None of them.

19

In those moments of tranquillity at night that swallowed up whoever they were during the day, they grew to sense the precariousness of everything they worked toward in the lighted world. What wait for (weight of?) love could ever counterbalance the edge they chose to live on? By gulping down still one more world in whatever fantastic shape each of them found it, they could feel something new developing. Sometimes the force of this energy turned them completely inside out and made them think that what they did during the night was what was most nourishing and protecting, and what they did during the day was so completely bizarre.

Commentary 5: Possibility

Fantasy

This chapter is about containment. It is also about issues of passion, entanglement, and renewal. And it is also about objectification and what happens when we try to "make data" like we "make love."

In the tradition of gothic romance, fairy tales, vampire chronicles, or recent renditions of daytime soap opera and bodice slasher (body snatcher?) novellas, the heroine yearns to escape her imprisonment within the well-guarded turret of her identity and find fulfillment in a passionate union with the forbidden other. In this kind of framework, we have two actors: an Eve, Rebecca, Rapunzel, or Princess Gina— seeking release as she traces her agonizing path through the labyrinth of the future— and the dark stranger, lover and devil, offering temptation, a redemption that is always just beyond one's eternal reach. At its core, it is the promise of the shining figure that bursts into the room and changes everything, and it is that moment we yearn for, that instance of connection, union, satisfaction, release. Yet we know that there is really no closure, that the story has no end. And we sense that this narrative will replay itself daily, in cycles of interruption and repetition resembling both the lives we yearn for and the lives we discard.

In many ways, this chapter sits at the intersections of gender, sexuality, and cultural studies where, within its fictional distance, relationships are identified as objects of study and the naming of personal life conquers the public, more masculine sphere. It is through the concerns of the personal— family, romance, sexuality— that the public sphere is represented. Perversely, the public display of the narrative makes privacy impossible and thus, through the collapsing of the private into the public, a violation occurs in the form of an uninhibited exposure of intimate information. As Peter Brooks (1976) suggests, it is a crisis of disclosure— nothing is spared because nothing is left unsaid. Personal narrative, in undermining standard research practice, becomes itself de-personalized, a kind of data for the (rock)pile.

In other ways, this chapter, through its fictionalized exploration of the longings, fantasies, and playings-out of heterosexual romance, promises a kind of resurrection, a new beginning, or sudden shift out of the patterns and templates of formal research relationships. Its melodramatic style, exaggerated interactions, self-referential suggestions, and sequential yet non-linear structure function in direct opposition to the (male) dominant ideologies of research practice and perhaps suggest the extent to which resistance is possible.

But in defying research convention in this way, have we really moved (beyond) the scripting of our academic world? When we wrote this chapter, we saw it as an interrogation of research relationships in academe. By disrupting, inverting, and then re-scripting the familiar romantic episode, we hoped to call to question the discourse of collaboration and the molding of its participants in specific roles. But in the end, the formulary of the genre held. The identities of both woman and man continue to be positioned according to the stereotypic discourse of want and need, desire and satisfaction.

But then again, who is really who in such dramas? How to account for the fluidity and transformations of identity? What remains is to interrogate the construction of each player's subjectivity outside the notion of a unified subject. Woman is never solely woman within masculine terms, never totally and permanently defined according to a male order. And man is similarly not inevitably bound by the constructions of his gender, or by any ideal which denies or imposes roles. In articulating the complexities of our own identities, embodiment, subjectivity, and in viewing them in terms of our collaborative work, we move (as Judith Butler, Joan Scott, and others have suggested) to reject the positioning of ourselves in terms of masculine universals or feminine specificities. But is this sort of positioning made inevitable by the genre of romantic fiction? Foucault (as discussed in Ahmed, 1998, p. 125), too, questions how the circulation of discourses may produce subject positions. If the value of this "fantasy" is in its portrayal of the struggle of self against the role, then the necessity lies not in the re-arranging and then re-imposing the romance, but in dislocating it from the discourses it invents . . . Or else, this chapter may be seen as still affirming "man-on-top" research.

Chapter Seven

Commitment's Tale
(Short Version)

December 20–22, 1997.

There is no "collaboration" between us anymore. (A Secret.) Maybe we really are two different people obsessed with doing what we want to do after too many years of doing what each of us thought we had to do together for whatever reasons. Maybe trying to be something we're not? Trying to write something we can't? Answer: You know me. And you?

Arranged to meet in Chicago this week to work on this chapter. Originally planned to write about the nature of this collaboration from a poetic, interpretive stance. But what can begin to symbolize the difficulties of the last months' research encounters in data form?

Anger, coldness, hate, and sorrow/
These [two] from each other borrow[1]

(To each they gave/From each they borrowed. . .)

None.

Walk up Michigan Avenue to clear our minds. Dead silence. Took circuitous paths to get together again to work at probably the worst time of year; and both of us know it's absolutely not working. It's not working at all anymore, at least not in the familiar, easy way that we've been accustomed to.

"something must ooze from the box, something will be perceived through the box or in the half-opened box . . ."[2]

Maybe it will look like a story. Maybe it won't, at least not in the usual sense. Maybe no one will believe it. It doesn't matter. Forget adding. Begin with attention. (A tension??) Forget the sense that things always have to happen in a certain way. Forget things always have to add up. Forget the fear. Begin with what happens at the precise moment of subtraction. Begin recording at this point. See what happens. Say what happens. The point when each of us has nothing to say to the other anymore, and when hearts have turned to bone.

"Hi."

"Hi. Plans have changed. I've got to stop in Beloit to drop off my grades. I didn't get everything done until last night. Want to have breakfast with me down there?"

"I thought we were going to work up there. I was just on my way up."

"It's the last day to turn them in. And besides, I can't stay as long as we planned. I couldn't arrange to get away for two nights. It's not as easy as it was out in California."

"I was just packing the car to drive up."

"I know. But I'm saying I can't do it like we said we would. Things change. Everything's crazy here. How about nine-thirty? At the Holiday Inn, at that coffee shop?"

"Is that a problem for you?"

In addition to the frustration of not being able to produce (to "get it up"? to "do it"?), we both sense a tremendous loss. The loss of the intensity and identity we used to share, and also that physical intimacy, gentleness, and affection. When did we each become so hard? Remember? We used to be like Scully and Mulder, a real team. Our friendship was so intense, so close that to imagine anyone, anything else being more important was impossible. When did we stop being number one for each other? When did it (you?) become so hard?

So many questions: Can we ever have control over our own work together? Over each other? From where and why do we feel the need to possess and exert such authority? What are we learning about collaboration (this impossibility) as a consequence?

And did we really have to take out all those other losses on each other? Or is that what real relationships are all about? (Sometimes it's comforting to know maybe you're not alone.) Must each experience be carefully extracted, so as to be eventually represented, maybe not as a central focus, but perhaps as one element in a relational field of a contemplating "imagination" . . . (not alone)?

Suppose the process of working together is a "complex weave."[3] Suppose it's like an art form, say, a dance, a movement, or a music that "breaks the circle of one."[4] Can two people collaborate together in "non-collaborative" ways in a "dumb" sense?[5] That is, can we conceive of an "innocent" exchange between/among our various (internal and external) selves where such exchange is "free" of dialectics and explication? Must our "working together" always have an object for its energy, or a form? Problem: Does breaking the circle of one create a new symbolic order that then becomes necessary to also break?

And then?

"Have the change?"
"It's still forty, right?"
"I think so."
"OK. Got it right here. Thanks. This the lane we want to be in?"
"Yeah, but everything's been changed around, so be careful, OK? Anyway, like I was saying, maybe it's not just an issue of representation. Maybe representation is less important to think about than the kinds of questions that these forms of data generate; that the display generates."

"Do they change the questions?"
"Right. Do they change the questions?"
"Give me an example."
"Remember the symposium on arts-based data display that Stephanie organized in Chicago last April?"
"Yeah, especially whoever did the intermedia work. That stuff really made an impact."
"What if you reversed the process?"
"Reversed?"
"If you focused on the questions these approaches generate, not the approaches themselves."
"I think I'm getting it. Say more."

If this is only coded language, do we learn it to say something other than what we mean, but which we both understand anyway?

I look up and see Jan coming down the escalator. I've already finished my coffee, and by the time she's made her way over to the table, the waitress is already filling her coffee cup, asking her what she'd like for breakfast. Jan picks up the menu, glances at it for a second, says, "Some breakfast rolls would be nice, and juice, please; grapefruit, thanks." Jan's eyes look tired, filled with sleep, and probably a thousand other things too. "It's so good to see you again, it really is," she says to me squeezing my hand, and then in the same breath, "What? Writing this down already?"

Two who write as one.

"There was no possibility of their agreeing on it. They would not even be talking about the same things; their vision would be of worlds that did not meet . . ."[6]

Sometimes it's so hard to imagine one voice matched along with another's. It really is, especially when the task may well be about shedding a lot of the ridiculous clothing that sentences need to fit perfectly, one word leading into the next with a kind of smoothness or certainty. Deleuze and Guattari speak (!) of a writing that "stammers" (!!!), writing that self-destructs. (Actually, we're watching this happening right now as we record these words on a paper bag from Au Bon Pain.)

(This good pain?) Then as you try to follow this idea through, sometimes it makes the act of writing more important than the object you think you're writing about (so you start again).

Perhaps corresponding to what Derrida, in referring to the psychology of collaborative writing (his wording: "écriture à deux mains"), likened to a voluntary state of hallucination, a mania; and not an epistemological experience.

"Remember the boxes I was looking for?"

"The boxes?"

"They're still missing. I found them once, but couldn't remember what was in them when I woke up."

"They've always been missing since I've known you."

"Sometimes everything is always missing."

"At least there's some continuity."

"When I was in L A last week, it was eighty degrees. Sun. The ocean was *so* blue."

"You called and left a message."

"No, I wrote you. I wrote you that I wished I knew what I was doing there. Or here."

"You wrote and called."

"I looked for just the right postcard to send. I sent you that postcard with a picture of waves smashing into the coast."

"Was that a postcard . . . or a metaphor?"

"Or a dream. The one I keep forgetting I'm in now. Then, too."

The difference between realize and analyze: we're more familiar with one than the other. What are the forces that drive us away from our truest desires?

"At this moment, it is not possible to define this space with any precision, nor will it be possible to describe it before entering it. The experiment in which we are engaged is a venture into this new space that awaits us."[7]

Wednesday night. Dinner at Tucci Milan in River North. For once, an easy, unintense, sequence of moments that last and give pleasure. Although it's been relatively mild all day today, when the sun set straight down West Hubbard, it set like a gunshot, and everything suddenly got colder, darker, older. But that was hours ago. Now, eight-thirty, and the restaurant is packed. Car lights flicker out the window on State. Hip (but not too) interpretations of nondenominational holiday music float over all the separated conversations like something actually sparkling and buoyant. Both of us seem startled by how all this works in a weird kind of way (by how we *want* it to work in a weird sort of way?) Question: When in collaborative time did we manage to dismiss these simple occurrences (nearness, intimacy of touch, softness of voice) as fundamental to our doing work together? When did we consciously begin to replace them for what we thought was important?

Among other things, some new theory subverts the status of the writer collecting data, writing alone. So new spaces open up, places for all kinds of relationships to emerge, where shared imagination can help us think and talk in different ways across difference for difference, and with much hope. With this may come new options for exploring the dimensions (and depictions) of experience, self-consciously and not; and it may be possible, OK, even, to experiment with untried methodological approaches: lyricism, for instance, or intimacy (to suggest two complicated examples), and then observe how these alternatives give new shape to research questions.

"If two become one, who is the one they become?"[8]

It hardly seems the same. The magic seems to flicker only in certain nights, when tiredness dissolves all pretense and certainty.

Used to be different. When did our calls stop starting with "Jan, I've got a terrific idea. You're really going to love this one."

When did we really begin working with(out) each other?

"Tears filled her eyes as she tried to fight off the knowledge that all this beauty and security could have been hers . . . She could have called this wonderful place her home."9

"Sometimes I wonder what would happen now if we just met."

"What do you mean?"

"At this time in our lives. Right now. By total accident. Today."

"What makes you think that?"

"I don't know. Just wondering. I was just wondering if things would work out differently. We're so different now. Would we begin to write together?"

"Would we begin to talk with each other?"

"Would we even *like* each other?"

"You're so different now."

"Maybe it's because I am."

"You're not the same person since Sonoma."

"You already said that."

"More focused. Clearer. Harder. You're tougher."

"People kept expecting me to be who I was."

"Maybe we all always want to be what we know."

"And I couldn't keep up with that fantasy. I couldn't keep being that anymore. I wasn't that person anymore."

"If you're lucky enough, you sometimes learn what's important."

"So I changed. It cost too much to not."

"I know."

"You've changed too."

"Surprise."

"Sometimes I really think Washington wasn't good for you."

"What do you mean, 'good for'?"

"That's *just* what I mean."

And then remembering this, "Keeping good field notes, making accurate maps, then 'writing up' the results" (and the systematic exclusion of a "subject at odds with itself")

is missing. One of the essentials, the development of the dialectic, is missing, One of the essentials, the higher level of generality is missing. One of the essentials, the hungry wolf in abstract form, is missing, One of the essentials, the episode where the young maiden and the prince finally get betrothed, is missing. One of the essentials, the sequence of fatal events on the way to grandmother's house, is missing. One of the essentials, the identity that substantiates the hero's true reference

The bus, as it fights its way through the rush hour traffic and the rain, things clear; two more hours, then home. Back to my world of familiar demands ("Pasta, Mom!" "Comma?" "Please."), easy transitions. Why, I wonder, if this is always so hard, why do I keep coming back to it? Every visit seems a betrayal, every phone call an accusation. And it only gets worse.

"Combined with this was another perversity . . . an innate preference for the represented subject over the real one: The defect of the real one was so apt to be a lack of representation. I like things that appeared: then one was sure. Whether they were or were not was a subordinate and almost always a profitless question."[10]

Late Friday afternoon. Snowing on the Mile and way out onto the lake. Sky gray as slate. Jan left yesterday to go back to Janesville to get ready for Christmas. I have mixed emotions about this. We just began to get past the crazy things, and now she's gone. Space to write, though, to get some of it all down, the intensity, before the mind says, "Hey, it's alright, loosen up, we all have our own load anyway." So I go shopping for presents for Lin in the Museum of Contemporary Art bookstore where I come across this vignette in the book *Making It Real* by Vik Muniz. The vignette: "A kid I know was watching the Oscars. When the actor Christopher Reeves came onstage he said, 'Everyone thinks this guy is Superman. I know who he really is. His real name is Clark Something.'" I put the book down and wander over to another display area. What something really is. I think about the "real" MCA on Ontario before this new MCA was built, and about what's missing in this new building, wedged in as it is between the Ritz Carleton and Water Tower Place. Get used to it: We really are different things at different times in our lives. Or at the same time. Where did I first come across the observation (and I'm paraphrasing wildly now, uncertain of the attribution) that without contradiction, our days are dreary and our life is so bleak?

"Come with me to Hawaii."
"Hawaii?"
"Come with me to Hawaii."
"Why? What's in Hawaii?"
"Sun. Time. Time for us. What we promised."
"Promised?"

"We promised we'd make a space for each other to celebrate *Daredevil* after it came out. Remember? Besides, the Early Childhood Conference is there this year. In January. We could leave New Year's Day."
"So . . ."
"So, let's go. We owe it to each other. You're on break anyway, right?"
"I'll be in Sarasota then."
"Do something different this year. Make a new tradition."
"If everybody's going to be in Hawaii, what do you mean 'time for us'?"

Maybe there truly is a moment that can be called "Dead Desire" even though both of us are working so diligently to deny it.

"The problem isn't so much with our lives, but with the linearity in which we've been taught to experience our lives. That's what I loved about my house in Madison. Everything was always happening at once. The real problem is how do we simultaneously allow for all that texture, all that richness, all that immediacy of our experience?"

Maybe the language that we need to create from this moment on (from here in this Chicago, this chaos today) is that we need to stop knowing as we did, stop thinking as we did, stop believing as we did, stop creating as we did. These notions aren't new and they need to be said even though they're immensely more difficult to practice. Still at least they may address (some of) the tensions that are separating each of us from what we have not been able to fully accept. Then there's Cixous, inviting us to enter her "School of the Dead."[11]

"Where are you calling from?"
"I'm at the MCA. You know, from one of the pay phones in the entrance area just underneath the stairs. Where we were yesterday."
"What's up?"
"Right. By the pool with the giant goldfish."
"I know. What's up?"
"I had to get as much of it down as I could. But then I couldn't do it anymore, so I'm taking a break. My stuff's in the café. I need to hear what you th ..."
"Getting what?"
"I was working in the café upstairs."
"What coffee? I can't hear you."
"Why don't you switch phones. You're breaking up."
"What?"
"Jesus, just give me a call back on a different line."
"Different *what*?"

At any moment, new research may emerge, creating radical, unexpected, localized projects for identifying issues for analysis and for developing agendas for social and other change. These projects may require alternative forms of exploration. Methods may become more diversified; and, in each location, with each new circumstance, will probably extend what is considered "best practice." (What should we expect of collaboration today?)

"Hey, Nick. Once we get connected and start talking, it's OK. We're OK. You know that? Nick? Hello?"
"Hello?"
"You're still there?"
"I'm here."
"What I mean is it's all these spaces in between."

Date: Mon, 26 Jan 1998 14:13:35 -0500 (EST)
From: jjipson@jvlnet.com
To: npaley@gwis2.circ.gwu.edu
Re: Chicago

Here it is. I really like it. Delete *italics*, add **bolds**. I didn't like your Sunday/Friday version. I'll call you. I'm going to the spa to celebrate.

Struggling to arrive at different understandings, they kept tearing apart what they felt, so they could get at what they felt, splitting images from words, separating specificities from totalities, then shuttling back and forth, making new experiences they could name or repeat like cuts from a record. Bits of things that grew between the lines. Like crab grass. Like the unexpected thoughts that develop inside your head in the middle of the night. Like the memories of the parts of some intact whole that no longer exists. (So will my heart be broken, when the night meets the morning sun?) Those kinds of bits.

"I know that you're gone, and you'll never come back. I miss you, but you're always doing something else, and it doesn't matter. Maybe if you lived five miles away, or even ten, things would be different. You could drive over every other morning in your new car, and we could really work together instead of doing this the crazy way we're doing it now. Or we could meet in some little pizza place like Pizza Gourmet off 101 in Cotati, and talk and feel like everything would be nearby and OK. Things would probably make more sense then. Things wouldn't be so fragmented. Maybe there'd be a better chance at making connections from one idea to another. The work would be real. More sincere. There'd be this close, safe, interpersonal space, and at least one of us would know what to say when the other had a question like, "How will anyone be able to use it?" or, "How will anyone be able to read it?" Yes, that would be so much better than this because distance would be divided in two; into two equal parts, and we could have a better shot at figuring out how to talk through the rest. So you wouldn't wake up in the middle of the night anymore staring at the edge of your face. You wouldn't have to feel like you were choking on your heart. But that's something that won't happen now. It won't come back. Nothing comes back. And it won't be real to try."

From somewhere far off, they sensed someone watching them work. Was it mom? As they deliberated about which path to take next, they imagined her smiling. Was this her way of letting them know that their efforts were on track?

Put Practice into Theory. (A different kind of climax)

Needing to look at things not always as examples of conflict or opposition, but as possibilities for invention and creative interaction. (Dewey)

delete all in italics.
ADD bolds.

"I can't even get you on the phone anymore. So I leave you a message."

"Again."

"Saying everything has gotten so much weirder, and stranger, more complicated."

"We don't even talk to each other in 'real' time anymore."

"Maybe once a month."

"Less."

"What's happened to us anyway?"

"Everything's so disconnected."

"Our schedules are so disconnected."

"Our lives are so off-key from each other now."

"Funny how it was so much easier to connect with each other when we were the farthest possible geographic distance apart."

"And now?"

"I teach a class. I get in the car, and . . ."

"I teach a class. I get in the car."

"Then I drive through hundreds of specific, ugly spaces that, you'll like this, all look the just same."

"In order to go someplace specific."

"K-Mart. I buy two tires. I pick up something to read."

"That's probably when I was trying to call you."

"And I'm probably picking up my messages from a pay phone."

"That's if I can even get through."

"A message from you about how you can never get through."

"About making these little portions to decorate something external that's no longer there."

"Decorate or van(qu)ish."

"There is no theory that is not a fragment, carefully preserved, of some autobiography."[12]

Were lonely and afraid and upset. Were lonely dream alone. Were afraid dreaming never together. Maybe only wanted love (like Yearwood). Maybe didn't bargain for this. Were blown away by now. Were change and complicit and confuse.

Didn't bargain for this,
You.

". . . the relations of things. It's like when you open a junk drawer and everything there including your hand, and your gesture, means something, has some history, of its making, and of its being there. Where the production of meanings is, if not continuous, so interconnected that one has the sense of, or the illusion of, the 'whole' of life being activated, and raised to realizations."[13]

Object of exhibition or struggle for liberation?

"The ending. It doesn't make much sense."
"What did you just say?"
"We seem to have lost the voices. Lost the dialogue."
"Are the voices the most important part?"

Even silence is part of the collaboration. Talk and silence. It's all there. It's all part of the collaboration. Such a large part of this never happens. It's never there. It always keeps happening, but it will never be there, and it will never always be the same.

"Every limit is a beginning as well as an ending."[14]

Why do I keep coming back to it?

"Hi, Nick. It's Jan. You must be out. Oooh, I just woke up from this amazing dream where I think I was disappearing. I was sleeping and I couldn't wake up and, uhh, I, yeah, everything was disappearing. Anyway, I was thinking a lot about what we've been doing and what's really important and who we are when we do this stuff together. If we just write what it all is, you know, no matter how disconnected, because that's what it is. That's what it all is. So don't you, or it, disappear like in my dreams, OK? Maybe I'll try to call you again later. Bye."

[Incompatible memory format]

[Unable to print this part]

NOTES

1. Lucy Ellman, Man or Mango? (New York, Farrar, Straus & Giroux, 1998), 56.

2. Gilles Deleuze and Felix Guattari, A Thousand Plateaus, trans. Brian Massumi (Minneapolis: University of Minnesota, 1987 [1980]), 287.

3. M. C. Bateson, Composing a Life (New York: Atlantic Monthly Press, 1990), 10.

4. Carol Mullen, M.D. Cox, C.K. Boettcher, and D.S. Adoue, eds. Breaking the Circle of One: Redefining Mentorship in the Lives and Writings of Educators (New York: Peter Lang, 1997).

5. Giorgio Agamben, Infancy and History: Essays on the Destruction of Experience (London: Verso, 1993).

6. Anne Perry, Rutland Place (New York: Fawcett Crest, 1993), 63.

7. Mark Taylor and Esa Saarinen, Imagologies: Media Philosophy (New York: Routledge, 1995), 1.

8. Guillermo Gomez-Pena, "The Free Art Agreement/El Tratado de Libre Cultura," in The Subversive Imagination: Artists, Society, & Social Responsibility, ed. Carol Becker (New York: Routledge, 1994), 213.

9. Mary Moore, Man of the High Country (New York: Harlequin, 1980), 64.

10. Henry James, The Real Thing. The Portable Henry James (New York: Penguin, 1892/1992), 110–111.

11. Helene Cixous, Three Steps on the Ladder of Writing (New York: Columbia, 1993), 1–53.

12. Paul Valéry, in Nancy Miller, Getting Personal (New York: Routledge, 1990), 1.

13. Rachel Blau DuPlessis, The Pink Guitar: Writing as Feminist Practice (New York: Routledge, 1990), 162.

14. George Eliot, Middlemarch (New York: Knopf, 1991), 881.

Commentary 6: Authoring
Commitment's Tale (Short Version)

Questions of genre necessrily provoke other questions about the complex relationship between the author and the text, and about the sites where meaning is produced. The author serves as an intermediary and the text is often the author's subjective production, linked interpretively, or not, to the reality of the experience.

In "Commitment's Tale (Short Version)," we surf across the unspeakable gaps between our stories, the dialogue in-transit, notes scribbled on café napkins, email messages, late-night dreams and inspirations— cutting cross-country over the scattered stenographic heaps of our work together. We assemble things, letting our experiences at the unstable borders between work and life write themselves as best they can, un-mediated by routine, convention, formula, analysis, or distance. As Deleuze and Guattari (1987) have suggested, "specific, unforeseen, autonomous becoming[s]" (p.106) emerge; there is no scenery to distract the eye, no intentional posturing or accumulation of sentiment, no self-censorship disguised by contextualization or interpretation— just the ambiguity of authorship. Reading becomes a process of disentanglement, an un-gnarling of the threads of the narrative.

But does the authorship really matter at all? What difference does it make who is speaking? On one hand, Roland Barthes (1979) suggests that "the author is never more than the instance of writing" (p. 145). The refusal of the ideology of authorship opens up the text to a plurality of interpretations, predicated on the opaqueness and complexity of the text itself, and the text becomes re-figured as "a multi-dimensional space in which a variety of writings, none of them original, blend and clash" (p. 146).

Conversely, Sara Ahmed (1988) encourages us to recognize the difference of the "who" that writes. She suggests that the who makes a difference, "as a marker of a specific location from which the subject writes" and that "the refusal to enter the discourse as an empirical subject [may] translate into a universalizing mode of discourse" (p. 125).

We struggle. But who is the we? Which version, what voice? Which part where, and in what order? Do these fragments, assembled so much by chance, author themselves? And where in these sentences are we still hiding?

Chapter Eight

Duplications

"Duplications" was inspired, in part, by *Storms* (1989, Mulberry Books), by Seymour Simon. Several passages of Simon's text were "duplicated" in developing this essay.)

Duplications are the most lethal storms known. They destroy more things on earth than everything else added together. Some duplications have the potential to extend over thousands and thousands of miles, and the destructive power produced by some of them is so intense, it is like a thousand lasers exploding at once. When duplications form, they exert tremendous pressure, moving with incredible speed until their force crashes against whatever is in their way. The resulting devastation can be awesome, and their effects can be felt long after they have disappeared from view. During the height of some of these phenomena, the violence is unreal, and the whole world howls in obliteration. At the center of most duplications is the eye— a clearly defined location of light and air so pure that it could almost be a symbol for something else. Inside the eye, everything is still as death, and the sun shines in a sky of clear blue.

Commentary 7: Another Kind, Another Sort
Duplications

How far can the possibilities of arts-based inquiry be pushed as part of the process of re-conceptualizing power? "Duplications" is an attempt to respond to this question from a postmodern perspective; and we see it as contributing to the increasingly rich, creative, and analytic experimentation by educational researchers working in this wider imaginative space. This specific effort was one of an extended series of our own arts-based interventions which emerged from a need to break apart familiar forms of discourse about educational research.

In some of these previous interventions, we experimented with creating such openings through the resources of media, text, and inter-text. Central to many of these explorations (but perhaps most intentionally explicit in "Duplications") was a twofold interest: to confront the oppressiveness of repetitive analytic structures and ritualistic research language, and to critique such efforts from perspectives which accessed the aesthetic, the visual, and/or the conceptual, and which themselves were always different.

But questions of duplication emerge everywhere, and no space is privileged from their sudden appearance. Working against historical practices and formulaic research rubrics that have often repressed individual need and imagination, "Duplications" results from an effort to employ practices that are of "another kind." But in so doing, does it only suggest containment of another sort? Walter Benjamin (as discussed in Levin, 1993, pp. 22-23) has analyzed modernity's obsessions with the visual image and visual productivity, seeing the world of late capitalism as "dominated, and haunted by, dream-images and commodified visual fetishes" that, according to Benjamin, "re-enchant[ed] the world which the Enlightenment, and then Marxism, had struggled to free from illusion." Peering behind these carefully calculated visual constructions, Benjamin saw an entire system of "exploitation, alienation, surplus labor, and power" which were masked by these productions. We wonder if we will recognize the moments when this happens in postmodern time, and how we will confront the illusions created by this form of ritualism. And we wonder whether the visual turn in our work actually contributes to seeing the world in any fundamentally new way at all—free from the duplications of the past—or if, by continually creating images, we only manufacture artifices, and duplicate the processes that Benjamin warned against.

Chapter Nine

Critiquing Collaboration: Fragmentation, Doubt

(Just) the two of us, engaged in producing and, too often, reproducing research, writings, and presentations, working together as teachers and friends for over twenty-five years. We have accomplished much, by some standards: co-authored several books and nearly a dozen scholarly articles, presented numerous papers at professional meetings, worked with students at our respective universities. And not unlike marriages or other intimate relationships, our work together has required perseverance, dedication, an ability to discern and adapt to each other's moods and life transitions, and a not insignificant degree of trust that our projects would work out in the end, that we would still like each other when they were over, if they were ever over. And, as in marriage and friendship, we have found that affection and forgiveness were key to the survival of our work life together.

But our collaboration has not always been the smooth, easy process we imagined it would be. Issues of personal boundaries, identity, and imposition have often intruded into our work together. We have learned that collaboration, difficult even under the best of interpersonal circumstances, is sometimes nearly impossible when connecting across long distances and great gaps of time. As we worked together, we found that each project seemed harder to finish than the last, each working visit seemed rougher, more painful. And yet, faced with increasingly insurmountable physical, temporal, and personal barriers to getting (it) together, we have persisted in doing collaborative work for many years. But why?

The Terrain of Collaborative Research

In this chapter, we reflect upon why and how we do research together and what we have learned about collaboration and relationships through this process. We look back at our earlier collaborative projects to map our developing collaboration and to provide a grounding for our current work. Several of these earlier pieces are included in this book as points of reference for our discussion (Jipson & Paley, 1991; 1992b; Paley & Jipson, 1997a).

In scanning across the ever shifting issues of personal identity and the irregular plane of our collaboration, we consider whether our research process was or could ever be truly harmonious, could ever equitably represent the separate and often distinct interests of each of us. Within the reality of our work together and the confusion of the identity issues we encountered, our collaboration took the form of multiple overlapping instrumental, conceptual, relational, and dialectical paths. It is this journey that we portray in this chapter.

Our current process of research reexamination has forced us to take a step back and away from the experimentation of our more recent work. We have begun to recognize our collaborative journey not as the seamless flow we liked to imagine it to be, but as a series of jerks, hesitations, incomplete gestures, the fragments of a lived relationship. Several challenges have faced us from the very beginning of our work together and continued to frame our discussions about doing research collaboratively. From our very first collaborative research project on the selective tradition in the elementary classroom, we have been concerned with what counts as valid and useful knowledge, and the issue of whether knowledge need be transformative. We began our initial study of the selective tradition by considering questions such as: What books did teachers read to their students or why did they make the choices they did? From what perspective could we analyze teacher responses? Who would construct the analysis? Using what vocabulary? Whose voice? As our work together progressed through subsequent projects on literature-based curriculum (Jipson & Paley, 1992a) and fiction as curricular text (Jipson & Paley, 1992b), we began to ask ourselves further questions: In what ways should our research findings be contextualized? How should they be constructed and represented? Later still, with the preparation of our first book, *Daredevil Research: Re-creating Analytic Practice* (Jipson & Paley, 1997), we began to consider other questions: Would our textual representations include artwork? Photography? Poetry? Dance?

But the questions we address in this book are ones we have continued to ask ourselves: What is the real nature of the relationship between collaborative researchers? What are the interpersonal dynamics of working together to produce "new knowledge" and "new forms of expression"? How can we, as collaborative researchers, adequately acknowledge and represent the multiple perspectives and understandings that emerge in a research process that includes two or more individuals, in our case, two very different people: male and female, Catholic and Protestant, urban situated and rurally oriented, exuberant and shy, single and maternal? The apparent oppositions (and the similarities) between us seemed to go on endlessly, both in our personal demographics and in our styles. How could we resolve the issues of boundaries, imposition, and power (Jipson, et al., 1995) so taken for granted in the generic research relationship, yet so vividly and painfully problematic in our own working together?

The Surface Piece

So, in the beginning, it was Nick and Jan. And that was even before the selective tradition, literature-based curriculum, or fiction as curricular text caught our interest. We saw ourselves, back then, banding together, helping each other out in the quest to find a stable place in the academic world. Our first projects were straightforward, tracing a trajectory toward certainty, toward knowledge, toward the answers to questions. Who reads literature anyway?

And which literature? And then, later, what role does the literary imagination play in the formation of identity? In understanding? In the construction of knowledge?

We read. We struggled to understand. And we wrote, paraphrasing and quoting what scholars had suggested before us when addressing the same questions, contextualizing our ideas within the frameworks of others. Back then, we were in complete agreement about our interest in how literature had assumed its increasingly central place in curricular thinking and classroom practice. We were both English teachers, after all, and curriculum theorists, too. We wanted to understand the phenomena we observed in the curricular repositioning of literature away from its role within the contemporary curricular canon, as an object for literary analysis. We wanted to clarify how standard "academic" textual materials failed to effectively represent the many ways in which the making of meaning takes place in social contexts, how such standard materials presented students with a limited view of culture, history, and experience. We wanted to affirm the notion that learning is not just the acquisition of unrelated skills and bits of information, but rather a process of constructing meaning that integrates new knowledge with personally felt experience. We wanted to assert that literature, with its focus on the personal, could offer a familiar face to material all too frequently presented in ahistorical, abstract form. And finally, we wanted to share our growing recognition of the power of literature as curricular text and the increasing integration of the literary arts throughout the curriculum.

In sum, we wanted to participate in the examination of the place of literature in the educational sphere, from textual politics to literature's role in the formation of teacher and personal identity and to fiction's grounding in pedagogy as curricular text. And almost before we could recognize what was happening, our initial study of the selective tradition had generated a series of other research projects, as one question led to the consideration of others.

The Identity Issue

In the beginning, we were very young. Almost children, we were starting out on our academic lives. We wrote about those early years: "We began working together in 1974 in a two-person education department in a small liberal arts college in southern Wisconsin. Our responsibilities ranged . . . ."

Even in our first projects on the selective tradition and on teachers' backgrounds for using literature-based curriculum, we were conscious of issues of interpretation and representation, although we did not label them in that way back then. Because of our earlier shared experiences as teachers and then doctoral students in the same programs, we assumed a great deal of complementarity between us. We liked each other and, in that, assumed we were also very like each other in most ways. Ironically, it seems now, as we discussed various interpretations of interview transcripts and questionnaire responses, we failed to fully acknowledge the differences in our own interpretations. We wondered if we really knew what the teachers we studied meant to say but assumed we understood each other completely. And in our excitement about the collaborative process, we constructed a merged identity. We became a "we."

It was eventually within this interpretive process, however, that we came to a more complicated understanding of the continually renegotiated relational issues of power and professional and personal boundaries, which seemed ever present between us. Although the overt form of each project seemed to emerge from the process of working together, the subsequent analysis and textual reconstruction of our findings were arduous as we interrogated each other's understandings, critiqued and corrected each other's words, and sometimes even questioned each other's commitment to the project at hand. Thus, the space between the idea and completion was painful, full of indecision and doubt. Was it because of a lack of trust in our own efforts? In each other's? Was it because of some kind of inherent yet disavowed competition between us? Between our competing sensibilities about what was "good" research?

Between our competing senses of who the other really was? Because somehow we needed to believe our work could be better if we worked side by side?

Although we thought of ourselves almost as a unitary collaborative entity, our focus on representation was totally external to ourselves. We debated about how we could accurately represent our interviewees' understandings of their own experiences without repeating, verbatim, all their words, and about how we could consolidate their experiences, and identify common patterns and motivations, without violating their individual meanings. We did not realize at the time that we were performing the same impositions on each other. The collaboration continued, intensifying through project after project, as we slid away from calculating numerical data and began to include extended informant quotations, and then entire autobiographic reflections, finally settling, not quite in desperation, on exploring our own personal-collective research process. And so we began writing about our work together, an autobiography of collaborative work. A collaborative identity?

"Surprised, but also delighted, by many of the parallels in our backgrounds, taking pleasure in our growing collaborations with each other across intellectual, instructional, and personal space," we wrote of our relationship with confidence. But at the same time, in our new focus on our collaborative self, we began trying to figure out just who we each were, and who we were to each other. And that has been the one thing that has remained constant across our friendship and our collaboration; we are still trying to sort through the identity issues in our relationship.

But back then, we continued to collaborate, separated by thousands of miles, yet in tandem, a sometimes self-defined "we," linked across our similar experiences as teachers and, hopefully, scholars. We had not yet really faced the sometimes brutal differences between us. We did wonder, when we wrote together, were we one or two? After all, in those initial years, we had chosen to think that we were pretty much alike. The surprises and dangers of blending and undefined boundaries had not yet occurred to us then. "Drawing on our undergraduate backgrounds in literature, we struggled to make spaces"; we wrote about "we" as if we were a single entity.

We realize now that everything keeps changing and that neither of us is the same person today that we thought we were yesterday. Just as we finally locate ourselves and each other, one of us notices that the other is in the process of becoming someone else. It is as if, as Judith Butler suggests, "identity is asserted through a process of signification, [and] if identity is always already signified yet continues to signify as it circulates within various interlocking discourses, then the question of agency is not to be answered through recourse to an 'I' that precedes signification" (1990, p. 143). The collaborative "we" that we thought we were seems now to have slipped away, if it ever existed in the first place, or outside of our separate imaginations. Again, Judith Butler writes:

> To qualify as a substantive identity [a "we"?] is an arduous task, for such appearances are rule-generated identities, ones which rely on the consistent and repeated invocation of rules that condition and restrict culturally intelligible practices of identity. The coexistence or convergence of such discursive injunctions (for instance, the injunction to be a particular race, class, or gender, or to be a teacher, or a researcher) produces the possibility of a complex reconfiguration and redeployment; it is not a transcendental subject who enables action in the midst of such convergence. There is no self prior to the convergence . . . There is only a taking up of the tools where they lie, where the very "taking up" is enabled by the tool lying there. (1990, pp. 144–145)

The Real Collaborative Work

The beginning of our actual research collaboration was in 1988 when we initiated the study of "The Selective Tradition in Teachers' Choice of Children's Literature: Does It Exist in the Elementary Classroom?" (Jipson & Paley, 1991). Concerned with issues related to literature and teachers' curricular decision-making, and with the political and positional dynamics encountered by practicing teachers, and working from our intertwined personal and collaborative histories, we were especially interested in the idea that books are not ideologically neutral objects, but that they both reflect and convey sociocultural values, beliefs, and attitudes. We sought to show that teachers, in the selection of books, were essentially selecting for or against specific kinds of cultural experience and images.

In defining our own relationship within the process of doing collaborative research, however, the unique personal characteristics of each of us created a complexity that became framed within the political concerns of power and imposition. Jan was, at core, a critical theorist, engaged in an examination of gender issues in education. Nick came from a similar academic tradition, with a focus on literature's place in curriculum. During that first project on the selective tradition, we made the predictable compromises. We would both collect data, using identical questionnaires. Nick would do the theory and lit review, Jan the data analysis section. We sidestepped potential conflicts over who would do what or whose perspective would prevail and "collaborated" on the project, each of us doing our own part at our own university and then meeting during the summer in Wisconsin to put the pieces together.

The Instrumental Issue

From an instrumental perspective, our division of labor made sense. After all, the traditional paradigm of empirical research, which we both had studied in graduate school, asserts that the world exists independently of knowers and that knowledge of the world takes the form of firm and steady truths that can be directly accessed through one's senses (Beyer & Bloch, 1996). Collaborative research just meant working together to answer the questions we had raised. Who did what did not matter. After all, research conducted within the traditional paradigms of positivism permits a finite range of research relationships that clearly articulate separations between researchers and researched and dictate the imposition of "objectivity" toward other research participants and the research itself. Perhaps we were still influenced by the belief that empirical research really could produce knowledge through detachment, knowledge which, because of its genesis, could be equated with truth, knowledge which was neutral and apolitical. According to this model, then, collaboration meant working with each other, but not necessarily together. We were interchangeable researcher-parts in the somewhat mechanical pursuit of "truth."

We sensed almost from the beginning, however, that this paradigm for research did not "fit" us and our philosophical/political beliefs. We had already discovered a complex range of interests, motivations, and relationships that we shared in our previous work together as teaching colleagues. We had never been entirely sure, from moment to moment, whether we were friends first or professional soulmates; but we did know that the fierce intensity of our regard for each other colored all of our interactions, including the professional. There could be no deliberate separation there, no objectivity. We shared interests, perspective, and intention in our mutual quest for academic and personal survival. Once we had abandoned our separate roles to achieve a more shared collaboration, working together became much more complicated as we debated interpretations, wordings, and first authorship.

The Conceptual Issue

It was at the conceptual level, perhaps, that our collaboration proceeded most smoothly. The long history of our relationship as colleagues, students together, and friends allowed us to understand each other easily, to think along the same lines. We concurred, for instance, in our critique of empirical researchers, agreeing that because of their (positivist) assumptions about objectivity and truth, they often failed to recognize the social and cultural valuing inherent in the decision as to what knowledges were most important to explore. We also agreed that they failed to consider whose interests were served by the knowledge they produced. And we agreed with each other that the positivist emphasis on instrumental features of observability, predictability, measurability, and generalizability as guidelines for the research process had a decidedly stultifying effect on researchers like ourselves, displacing or muffling their (our) recognition of the atypical, unpredictable, and idiosyncratic experience. Together, we affirmed the importance of recognizing those unique and emergent occurrences of lived experience rather than focusing on the identification and valorization of the predictable. We shared from the early years of our own educational histories a commitment to the creation of knowledge that is inexact, unexpected, and multi-focused.

There were several other areas of shared understanding that impacted our research and our collaboration. We agreed that knowledge is socially constructed and mediated and that it is invariably culturally and historically embedded in the concrete specifics of its situation. We shared the belief that knowledge must always be (re)viewed in the context of its constitution. It was this understanding, in part, that led us to our method for doing our second project, "Is There a Base to Today's Literature-based Reading Programs?" (Jipson & Paley, 1992a). Already slipping away from empiricism, we abandoned the necessity of acquiring geographic representation and numeric balance in our sample. We decided it was appropriate, instead, to work directly with the teacher education students at our own universities, asking them to share extended narratives about their reading habits. By focusing on the narratives, we hoped to better understand the relationship between their personal literary backgrounds and their curricular practices.

During our research on literature-based reading programs, we talked a lot about "objective reality," and how it actually could be whatever one's mind constructs. Each participant in our study had his or her own distinct reading history. Each of them understood, in their own unique ways, the relationship between their personal reading habits and their teaching. We found that they did not conform to facile categorization or distinctive and easily identifiable patterns, each made their own sense in their own way. Our interpretation of the data we had collected on their reading "bases" pulled away from the making of generalizations. The data was too complicated for that. The knowledge we gained was also too complicated for codification.

We began to articulate to each other our own beliefs about what counts as knowledge. From Jan's perspective, knowledge is valued in terms of its potential to contribute to progressive social change and social justice. Jan saw value in postmodern representation mostly as a political tactic, aimed at the undermining of other privileged, more empirical regimes of research. Nick worked toward the accomplishment of social transformation through the nonconventional approaches of literature and art.

We agreed, however, that knowledge is unequally distributed and that knowledge makers inevitably use their knowledge to enhance their own status and to support their own interests. For both of us, the knowing individual is one who can shape and reshape the world through her/his action, through symbolic and communicative activity, and through the dialectical interplay between the two. Most important for our continued collaborative work, we both believed that our academic world could be reshaped and transformed through human action. We knew this firsthand, since both of us were directly experiencing the mechanics of the knowledge-producing industry of academe where research output is inextricably tied to promotion, tenure, and success and where our combined efforts offered promise of at least partial success. Through our discussions, we had begun to understand that we, too, as academic researchers, were a kind of "colonized subject" in Western society, living our lives within and through the codes of our institutions and colleagues.

The Relational Issue
Our collaboration continued. In our next study, "Fiction as Curricular Text" (Jipson & Paley, 1992b), we chose to look at the dynamics of literature and

curricular decision-making from an increasingly more narrative and autobiographical perspective. Seeking an alternative to the constrictions of generalizability and objectivity inherent in more empirical research, we selected research processes which would allow us to focus closely on diverse voices and extended narratives, including, at some point, our own. We chose to interview colleagues from several universities about their use of fiction as text in their teacher education classes, but the interviewees' stories often extended into long personal accounts of their lives. Initially, by focusing on the particulars of our participants' narratives, we attempted to understand the meaning of events and interactions in their situations, from their point of view. The expectation that we could analyze and reconstruct what they had told us led us to believe that we could "recover" their personal realities, thereby developing new concepts of experience and providing insights from which we could refine existing knowledge about the relationship between literature and curriculum.

Reflecting on the interview data by phone, however, we began to share autobiographic information about ourselves and our use of fiction as curricular text in our own classrooms. This discussion prompted us to include our own experiences as part of the study, although we were unsure of the "legitimacy" of doing so. We came to see it, however, as an affirmation of our commitment to a research interactivity that was egalitarian and nonexploitative, one that promoted reflexivity as a strategy shared by all participants in the research process, including ourselves. We then began to focus our analysis on the intersubjective processes through which meaning, and thereby knowledge, is generated. Believing that when people interpret and make sense of their worlds, they understand from the subjective point of view of their own participation within their own cultural and interactional contexts, we increasingly felt it important to ground the study in our own personal and subjective understanding of literature and curriculum, a world we had shared as long as we had known each other.

Throughout those days, and even sometimes now, what we learned about each other, about our work, and about the world really did not exist separately, for the other was always a part of each of our worlds, either in connection or counterreaction to ourselves. The fiction as curricular text project became the center of our lives, and we found it extending into our classroom teaching and our conversations with friends. And even as we asked our interviewees to share memories, feelings, hopes, we also shared everything— pain, loneliness, fear, frustration, and joy, too.

We grew closer, visited each other often. It was as if our personal lives and our research merged, producing truths both transient and intuitive, truths that disappeared just as we noticed them— a glint of recognition, or a flutter deep inside our beings. We felt ourselves often not only outside the finite range of expected research relationships but beyond the shadow of relationship itself. Often, there was no clear distinction between us, no tolerable detachment, no knowledge or feeling which was not deeply personal and shared. Often, too, we could not remember who thought or said things first. Truth, it seemed, and experience belonged to both of us at once; and the boundaries between them, as between us, were often indistinct, below the surface of our collaboration.

The relational issue of imposition, however, an issue that Janet Miller (1990) has written about, kept recurring, particularly in our increasingly autobiographic work. We each realized that, just as in research, the assumption that we could always be cognizant of each other's motivations and agendas was faulty, and that our imposition of understanding or interpretation on each other often "created" rather than mirrored, the other's experiences, thoughts, and feelings. Neither of us could ever actually capture the other's lived experience, we discovered, in part because as soon as the experience occurred it was gone-- except through its (partial) (selective) reconstruction in each of our memories and later in our writing. Thus, we began to recognize that in our work together it was our separate recollections that were being imposed upon experience and that our research representation was, therefore, a narrative production rather than a narrative reproduction. The only story we could tell was our own. The growing problem was, however, that we did not share the same story.

The lack of clear boundaries between us as researchers and friends sometimes clouded our recognition of differences between us, and the closeness of our long-term relationship led us to unwarranted assumptions about each other and each of our core feelings and beliefs. Ultimately, our co-identity as collaborative researchers was shaken by these recognitions, and we are still struggling to understand the assumptions that we each make about the relationship between what we experience and our individual interpretive systems. Differences in our professional preparation, our social and regional backgrounds, our family-historical experiences, and our cultural traditions often generated differences in our understanding of each other and our data, and thus constituted a barrier to our collaborative attempts at representation, particularly when we were not working side by side. For example, Nick was immediately comfortable with using graphic and photographic images to represent concepts and experiences. Jan remained primarily oriented to textual representations but began to experiment with the design and composition of print text on the page. Accommodating differences such as these into a non-unitary collaboration became our new challenge.

Emerging Dialectical Issues

With our work on our first book, *Daredevil Research* (Jipson & Paley, 1997), we began to more clearly acknowledge the difficulties implicit in our roles as collaborative researchers. Interpretation, by its very definition, implies the possibility of multiple understandings, multiple meanings for every idea or event, and we often held very different positions. We debated, argued, sometimes even sulked as we attempted to impose our personal interpretation on each other. And yet we often agreed that there were many reasons for preferring one explanation or interpretation over another, reasons that sometimes had little to do with the data. We began to recognize that even when we could not agree on a preferred meaning, each of our alternate, sometimes impressionistic representations served to inscribe power and value in specific ways, thus creating particular social texts and engendering particular possibilities. Multiple representations merely obscured the issue. Whose multiples and in what proportion?, we argued. Finally we agreed that collaboration in postmodern times really was risky business. It was at these times that we felt the heavy weight of modernist responsibility slowly re-descend upon us as we retreated to an invocation of convention and an imposed univocality.

Inseparable from the troubling issues of privilege and value inherent in our actual research was a parallel set of concerns questioning the politics of conducting research outside our own shared experience (Hauser, 1998) and of researching individuals, other than ourselves, at all (Jipson, et al., 1995). Central to these concerns was our shared belief that authentic depictions of subjective experience could be generated only through personal reflection on one's own lived experience and the frequently intuitive examination of one's own ideas and beliefs. The one thing we still shared was our collaborative work. But what of our many non-collaborative experiences? What about the ideas that awakened one of us in the middle of a solitary night? How did they all fit in? What, then, was our role as collaborative researchers, and how were we to do research at all?

We found ourselves moving toward a research of our own personal experiences with collaboration and our own teaching practices. And yet we realized that each of our shifts from the established traditions of grounded understanding to methodologies respecting personal perspective and voice and representations that were ambiguous and deeply personal was risky for a variety of reasons— the exclusion of other than our own personal experiences being the primary issue we considered at the time.

We saw, however, our movement toward personal co-narrative as contributing to a reformulation of our research and textual politics. Acknowledging the influence that fiction and poetry has had in our own understanding of ourselves and our educational practice, we began to increasingly integrate these genres throughout our teaching and research. In our teaching— fictional, poetic, biographic, and artistic voices spoke alongside each of our own. In our scholarly work, these same voices interrupted our thoughts and our writings, inserting themselves literally into the very texts we were producing.

We struggled still, however, with issues related to the "legitimacy" of what we were writing, Was it narcissistic to examine our own teaching? Or self-absorbed? Was it too self-congratulatory to write about our own experience? Were we being exclusionary, invoking the very same selective tradition we had earlier critiqued? Was all of our research merely autobiographic? We wondered, were we merely reproducing, duplicating ourselves and our experience over and over again?

Concerned, we reconsidered Britzman's suggestion that we turn the focus of our research back upon ourselves, deconstruct ourselves, "unraveling the myth of narrative omnipotence and thus the fiction of the unencumbered self" (1995, pp. 150–151). We struggled to understand just who we were becoming as collaborative researchers. We came to feel that only through our varied experiences with each other and the co-creation of personal narratives across time could we construct a sense of our collaborative self, and then only for the briefest moment before it renewed itself.   Resonating with Miller, we questioned whether we should turn our back on theory, on politics, in order to speak with a nonacademic voice. In "the splitting off of 'private life' and the merely 'personal' from conventional academic discourse" (Miller, 1991, p. 5), had we, in fact, betrayed our commitment to classroom teachers, to curriculum reconceptualization, to a "real" kind of political engagement, and to each other? Had we shrouded our emerging counter-narrative of resistance beneath our personal obsessions? Yet these questions had led us to an analytic practice that pushed us beyond established research protocols, to a breaking down of barriers between subject and object, to an obliterating of boundaries between researcher and researched, between friend, lover, and colleague. We found ourselves thrown back and forth between the powers of the various positions we considered.

Pummeled by the roaring hurricanes of our ever-emerging understanding of ourselves and of the research process, we continued to experiment with questions of knowledge production and representation. Attempting to be sensitive to both institutional research expectations and our own personal traditions of research, we found ourselves variously immersed in feminist, post-structuralist, and critical art theorizing. We began to more actively experiment with different ways of representing "data," employing unconventional and, to us, unexpected genres, textual designs, and representations. "Personal History: Researching Literature and Curriculum (literal, alter, hyper)" (Paley & Jipson, 1997b), which is presented as Chapter 2 in this book in a revised form, is reflective of these theoretic and personal shifts as we let chance become a coproducer of our research report. Working through interchanging sets of theoretical frameworks, increasingly responsive to the imperatives of post-positivism, we continued to experiment with nontraditional forms of textual representation and began to consider how we might apply strategies of imaginative construction, discontinuous cadence, polyphonous voice, and bricolage to our current work. Out of this exploration came "Curriculum and Its Unconscious" and "Method Who Am I?" which we included in our first book together, *Daredevil Research* (Jipson & Paley, 1997). In a sense, we had begun to reveal what Clandinin and Connelly (1996) describe as the sacred, the cover, and the secret stories of our collaboration.

Issues of Fragmentation

As we began to think about our collaboration less as separate "studies" or as simply the basis for the articulation of our "multiple voices," we began to see it more as an inter-textual, dialectical collaboration that could provide an alternative to both established, formal ("sacred") research reports focusing primarily on the representation of "major knowledges" (explanations and answers, data and results), and to research narratives offering personal anecdotes and reflections (the "cover" story) on the doing and writing up of research.

Recognizing that diverse, hidden, yet important understandings or "minor knowledges" (contradictions, challenges, ambiguities, disconnections, disagreements, and displacements) might be overlooked in these official narratives of research, we began to create texts such as "Duplications" (Paley & Jipson, 1997a), "Animals and Curriculum Masters" (Jipson & Paley, 1999) and this book, *Questions of You*. These texts revealed what we understood as the "secret" story of research: the ambiguity, the pain, the repetition, the confusion. In juxtaposing and colliding the finished with the open-ended, the composed with the repetitious, end results with subjective experience, conclusions with no beginnings, fact with fiction, cohesiveness with incompleteness, authority with autonomous voice, order with the random, and the personal with the rubric, we finally gave ourselves over to the representation of the hidden, the painful, and the confused. Our research was never more creative. Our collaborative relationship was never more contentious.

It was inevitable, perhaps, that with our co-abandonment of notions of progress and the unitary self (Bloom & Munro, 1993) we would also experience nearly fatal fractures within our own collaborative relationship. Across the years, our separate lives had become more complex and our individual priorities had necessarily adjusted to balancing our roles as collaborative researchers with our personal lives, and also with our varying commitments to social change and our differing understandings of the social construction of meanings. We found ourselves admitting that we were no longer necessarily as central to each other's life as we once had been, that despite our years of collaboration, our identities were (still? again?) separate and distinct. Or was it that as we thought and wrote about the secret, messy, and contradictory process of doing research today, we began to first acknowledge those same qualities in ourselves and in our relationship?

The inherent conflict in being committed to a liberatory, reflective, narrative-focused research, while not imposing personal values and agenda on others, raised serious issues for both of us. What was impositional to each of us? On each of us? Where were each of our boundaries of propriety? Of availability?

Of expense? Whose meaning or sensibility counted? Counted most? Whose schedule counted most? When? We had grown to depend on each other, on our differences, to be what we thought was a "complete" researcher. We delighted in locating things the other had not read, in coming up with novel ideas, in finding just the right word or phrase to express an idea. Had it become a competition of sorts? Were we once again, or had we always been, separate individuals? Was our collaborative identity merely a compromise in the name of respect and affection, or of production, more than anything else?

The questions for us as research collaborators were insistent. How could we share each other's reality when it was continually changing? How could we more directly engage each other in our separate processes of meaning making and knowledge producing when we continued to live several thousand miles apart? How might we do this, given the inherent positional power and gender/class status of each of us, things which seemed to so readily overwhelm and subvert the other's understanding of her/his own experience and agency?

We learned much. We learned that collaborative research must begin with intersubjective understanding and commitment between participants. We learned that the doing of research, however, constructs boundaries, boundaries which can enable or constrain relations of power related to discourse, culture, location, and subjectivity. At various times, we have questioned each of these. We still do. And we struggle still with issues of what commitment means in our relationship, of what is represented by understanding. And we struggle still with power.

Is the challenge for us in our collaboration, then, to locate and ground our research in the interpretations and understandings we share and to distinguish between the multiple interpretations we consider, recognizing that subjective understandings are ever partial? Through an ongoing process of critical reflection, must we develop an awareness of how our separate understandings and impulses may have been distorted or repressed or may have contributed to the understandings we construct together?

Research can also be about the process of constructing representations of our understandings, representations we sometimes call knowledge, sometimes art. How do we choose to represent our understandings if all of our experience, and therefore all of our knowledge, is under continual construction/reconstruction? What purposes do our partial, shifting, positional representations serve, particularly if they are only amalgamated representations of our own separate realities anyway? Or can collaboration really occur at any other level? And what about all of the personal issues that arise, that continue to arise? Boundaries, imposition, identity, power— are these the essentials for doing collaborative research after all?

The Final Part

And so we ask, as co-participants in the inquiry process, what counts as research? What matters as data? What procedures are considered legitimate, ethical for the production of knowledge? And how can we, together, contribute to the making of meaning?

How can we interrogate knowledge itself in terms of the social and historical context of its production? Similarly, we must ask ourselves how our past research has been constructed and how it can be reorganized or reformulated into an analytic existence that acknowledges our co-participation in its process, including the process of representation.

But there are also other questions. Why should we do research at all? Why not just be friends, companions? Should production or performance be more important than friendship? Is writing books really more important than sharing a bottle of wine or driving up the coast to Mendocino on a sunny afternoon? Why should it be? Can we assume that there is actually "new" knowledge to discover anyway? And how do we determine what knowledge is worth the time of its "discovery"? The loss of time? Is "new" knowledge really just an application of an old story to a new situation? Or, since all knowledge is grounded in personal experience, is "new" knowledge just a shifting of interpretations as they are layered on life across time?

As we struggle to examine our collaborations—and our experience, work, productions, process, obsessions, and identity—we are reminded, by Sandra Harding's (1987) search for a distinctively feminist methodology, that perhaps what the practice called collaborative research needs is a rethinking of familiar research methods, a movement beyond replacing objectivism with subjectivism and intersubjectivity, beyond assessing generalizability and particularity, beyond debating truth and relativism. Needed, perhaps, is a close examination of the constructed and dialectical nature of collaboration and the invention of new researches where multiple understandings of experience can flourish, where separate and connected voices can be heard, and where the historical and sociocultural contexts in which we live today can be central to our understanding.

Commentary 9: Theorizing

Critiquing Collaboration: Fragmentation, Doubt

Although, for the most part, we have situated the chapters in this book within the historical trajectory of our work together and have implemented, as a frame for our co-analysis, a postmodern representational schema, this project seems to, in and of itself, also necessitate a meta-review of its own political and conceptual development. The ninth chapter, "Critiquing Collaboration: Fragmentation, Doubt," constitutes our efforts to re-call such a scholarly analysis of our collaborative projects. Thus, while in present time the majority of our collaborations are represented within the context of postmodernism, we assert here our need to undertake a formal, critical analysis of how modes of research production and representation may alternately restrain or enable social and personal transformation.

Within our developmental analysis and from the shared perspectives we bring as collaborative researchers, we have employed strategies of rupture, inter-text, and multiple representation to expand our analysis of the social and cultural dimensions of research identity and practice. And through this seemingly endless theorizing and re-theorizing, layering and re-layering, positioning and escape, we hope to return the personal to the sphere of the political, to re-construct our personal research experience within the larger discourse of what Norman Denzin (1995) calls the double crisis of the social sciences: representation and legitimation (p. 35).

In creating the "social text" of this chapter, we directly participate in naming the relationship between the lived experiences we shared as collaborative researchers, the experiences we "lived" in co-authoring this book, and the "intentional meanings" we created in Chapter 9 and in our inter-textual commentaries. When we, as subjects of our own research activity, choose to represent ourselves, and in creating these representations and commentaries, reveal ourselves yet again, our intention is, in fact, to live-out our experience before our readers' eyes. Following Denzin, the textual (re-)production of our discourse and, in particular, Chapter 9, both creates our experience and, at the same moment, transforms it into something that no-longer, ever occurred. As Denzin (1995, p. 40) suggests, "there can never be a final, accurate representation of what was meant or said, only different textual representations of different experiences." In its cycling through our understandings of our work together, and in its multiple forms, we intend this chapter as a discourse which refuses to "ignore who we are collectively and individually" (Racevskis, 1983, p. 20, as cited in Denzin, 1995, p. 41) and which situates us and our text squarely back in the political world.

Chapter Ten

Castaways

February 20, 1998
Rockford, Illinois
I get out of the car and walk across the parking lot. It's 4:20 p.m. When did they put up this Fairfield Inn? Or the Ramada directly across the highway from the new Wal-Mart Super Store? During what period of darkness did all the morphing of this landscape take place? Or was it my own? My own lack of notice? Once, years ago, when I grew up right here in the middle of this particular part of the Midwest, I remember how there was such wind and red wheat and sky. The seasons would come and go, and my dad would teach at the college and my mom would work in the catalogue department at Sears. This seemed to go on forever, just like all the winter fields and cornstalks in the snow. Catholic school. Hand-picking corn each June and July on Colley farm that didn't get harvested the autumn before. Six to noon for five dollars a day. On this cold, mid-February Friday afternoon, everything seems so completely different and new. I walk into the lobby and ask the receptionist where the pay phones are. I dial up the access code and wonder whether to punch in Jan's

number to leave a message. What would I say that she hasn't already heard? That all this has gotten too far away from where we started? That it lacks anything useful or real? How would she answer differently anyway? Not new. Earlier this afternoon, before she got on the Van Galder bus to Janesville and halfway through our second beers at Tumbleweed Bar and Grill, she asked, "So, do you ever think we'll work together again?"

The voice on the audex beeps in. "You have eighteen messages." I begin to take down the first four names and numbers in my notebook, then fast forward through the rest. What is the sum of one day's desire? Who is to say what is surface and what is depth? And for whom? Thoreau, during his trampings through the New England woods, made much of his understanding, if we can believe his accounts, from what he experienced, from the kinds of wilderness he encountered daily. That was his research. That was his collaboration. His dialogue. And even then there were moments of deeper wilderness, and he did not know: "Walden," he once whispered, "is it you?"

I walk back to the car and get in, then turn onto the access road to head east on 20. Questions shiver in the trees I live in, telling me something. I keep the tape recorder on, trying to hear the things that are hidden behind words, hidden by words. What can we really know? What can we truly hear? Will we dare speak it? Each question seems like a box, leaving a message, turning into bags and puzzles for me. The light turns green, but nothing's moving. Waiting in traffic, I can feel my mind drift. What do we choose to write about when we record? What do we leave out? When is data collection time ever over? I think of Jan on the bus, maybe reading or looking out the window at the huge world. This outrageous struggle to make things real, make things as transparent as you possibly can through your own language, your own understanding, and not by precedent alone . . . so to make things change. But maybe when you're looking for a key, you sometimes find something else. Then what you lose, do you gain by accident? I punch the radio on and hit seek, which scans the signals of what is, then locks onto the last part of an old Bob Seger song: ". . . just livin' to run, and runnin' to live . . ." I think of how Jan likes her newest new home. I think about the new hopes she has and how she talks about them with such belief and enthusiasm, even as she did in California before much of it fell away. Or Oregon before that. Ten, twenty years (against the wind?) to return to the half-pretty, industrial towns on the Rock River where we started. Then a split second and I blink. As if this is who we are.

* * *

Summer, Sonoma County, 1994

I find myself in the backyard, wine red juice staining my fingers as I fight the brambles for the blackberries. It is the third time since July that I have caught myself picking berries, making pie, while my academic projects sit in the computer. The berries, I know, won't wait, and the greater loss seems to be to let them go to waste. I am intuitively clear about what counts as real work: picking berries, making pie or jam. The writing projects seem endless, particularly on this beautiful July day, and sometimes I'm not sure they count for much at all in this land of so much wealth, of so much poverty. It makes me wonder: what am I doing with my life, an academic in California where people hire other people to care for their gardens, to clean their houses, to raise their kids? Get real, I say. To myself?

Summer, Wisconsin, 1995

Home again. Glen Flora. Wisconsin to California and then back. I sit at the bedroom window in my father's "new" house and look out across the field to the house where I grew up, and beyond that, to Snag Hill and the remnants of my great-grandparents farm. Quite a journey. From farm fields to what my students call "the knowledge factory," certainly a trip I had never intended to make.

Just an hour ago, I was sitting at the kitchen table with my aunt, talking of berries, tomatoes, and making pie. I think about our conversation, how effortless it seemed and how gratifying, a natural language where I needn't worry about interrupting or think about choosing the right words; the kind of talk and the kind of life that still remains first in my mind across many years as an academic and as a writer. It's good to be back.

Summer, Glen Flora, 1997

We scattered my dad's ashes on the Flambeau yesterday. The cabin seems different in the early morning light. No familiar voice calls from up the hill, telling us of his arrival, warning us to get up, quick, and get the coffee on or we'll miss the best part of the day. I make the coffee anyway, hang his backpack and fishing hat in its familiar place next to the kitchen door, promise myself we'll never change a thing about this place in the woods which now seems like the only "real" home I have left. In many ways, it seems like the end of the life I knew in northern Wisconsin. What are left are just mementos, like the mounted deer horns and the fishing hat, which call up the memories, and the stories, and the dreams of a way of life that will be part of me forever.

Memories. Northern Wisconsin

I learned about working early on— and about the kind of life I still think of as real. My parents had grown up during the depression in northern Wisconsin. My grandparents taught them (and me) to harvest every ripe berry, to slice and can each tomato, to pass down the faded tee shirts and battered toys from child to child, family to family. As a young child of nine and ten, I picked wax beans for Stokley Van Camp for two cents a pound. Long, hot days in the fields working with other women and children from my community and from the migrant camp down the road. Speed was essential: the more you picked, the more you earned, but it was also very important to "pick clean" so that the owners hired you back. We created competitions for who could make the most in a day, three or four dollars if you were good, and rewarded ourselves with drawn-out lunch breaks in the shade of someone's pickup, sharing warm, red Kool-ade and peanut butter and honey sandwiches until we were told it was time to get back to work.

I often stayed at my grandparents' farm as a young child while my mother taught school in one neighboring community or another. I liked to get up early to eat a bowl of oatmeal with my grandfather before he went back out to clean the barn. In the spring, I helped him pick rock, string barbed wire around the pastures, and tap sugar maple trees for sap which my grandmother would boil down into maple syrup. Sometimes we would pour the hot sap on the snow to make candy. We reminded each other of the "right way" to do it, dripping the sap at just the right speed so that it would ball up in the snow.

In winter, the men would hunt, first partridge and pheasant, later deer. My sister and I would go with my dad, at first to escape the household chores, later because we enjoyed the camaraderie of hunting camp. My grandfather, who had once worked in a logging camp, was the designated butcher, gutting the deer, hanging them in the shed to age, cutting them up into chops and roasts, grinding venison sausage. Once I dreamed that the deer carcass hanging in our cellar to age was my pet. The next morning when I went down to throw coal in the furnace, I was surprised my deer was not really alive.

There was always work on the farm. I helped my grandmother candle eggs to take to the store in town to sell; egg money was my grandmother's own to spend. Sometimes I was allowed to sprinkle lime in the gutters after the men had cleaned the barn. Other times, I would watch my grandmother cut paper dolls from a newspaper, help her make cookies, or cuddle up on her lap and listen to her stories of first coming to Glen Flora on a boxcar. Once, walking up the trail from our cabin to the road, a wolf crossed our path and she comforted me with stories of the wolves and bears that were part of her childhood landscape. I began to think of myself as Laura in the Big Woods.

Early fall was the busiest time, blanching beans, tomatoes, and peaches for canning and skimming the sweet foam off the top of the jam as it boiled. What I did not like was chasing the chickens across the yard so that my grandmother could butcher them. I remember it all: how the ax slashed down through the hen's neck as it was held to a stump, the headless bird dancing away across the yard as if it were still all there, and the cleaning and plucking of the chickens, my sisters and I constantly reminded by our mother to get all the pin feathers off or we'd find them in our soup.

And then there were other times, too, other realities that intruded on my childhood understanding of the world, Sunday school, for instance, where everything seemed to be a contradiction but where I learned to win the prizes for memorizing Bible verses. School itself seemed insignificant, no "real work" was involved, just made-up activities to keep kids busy: penmanship drills and dull stories about children who lived in white houses with picket fences and sidewalks; a fourth grade assignment to write a thank-you note. Frustrated after completing my third or fourth unacceptable draft, I told my teacher I had already written a thank-you note and mailed it from home. My mother was furious at my lie. Seventh grade: writing an essay on what conservation means to me, I tried to translate what I knew about ploughing and terracing and picking rock into the language that eventually won me the prize, a Labrador retriever that I named Rex. Was winning the prizes what counted?

Summer, Janesville, Wisconsin, 1998

Once more I anticipate a long overdue reunion with Nick. We have promised each other that this time we will take time together, drink beer, watch the sunset from the Union Terrace. We have assured each other that this time we will create an oasis, we will celebrate the friendship that has sustained us across so many projects. And, inevitably, we will work. Finish this book, anticipate a new project, write proposals. Real work. And hard work.

I'm back in Janesville, where I first lived in 1971 before life became real and I had to grow up. It's where my daughters were born, where I first began my professorial life. Where Nick and I first began to work together, became friends. Life in Janesville today is a life I think I understand, even if only as a nostalgic re-creation of the life I sometimes thought I lived before, the life I still now want to live. I've found yet another old house with a big front porch, wood floors, large rooms with angled ceilings and huge open windows. I've planted another garden: roses, lilacs, pansies, and potatoes and peas. My books are once more arranged on the shelves of my study and family pictures hang on the walls. And I teach. Illinois this time, but the students are much the same, small town teachers hoping to make a difference in their students' lives. But now, I also write books, use other people's words. I think a lot about where my work fits in the larger scheme of things, wonder about whether it has any real value, whether it needs to have any real value beyond the day-to-day.

Nick calls, reminds me that this chapter is due, overdue actually. He'll be out in a couple of weeks, when he returns from Brussels. We'll finish putting this book together, have a glass of wine to celebrate. Maybe we'll drive back to Milton College one last time and reminisce about how we first began to work together. He'll tell me that I am romanticizing my life. And he'll marvel at how I can come back here, where so little has changed in twenty-five years. I'll puzzle at why he stays away from this life here, in these "half-pretty, industrial towns on the Rock River." We'll walk by the river and I'll remind him, again, that this is who we are.

Achebe, C. (1959). *Things fall apart*. New York: Astor-Honor.

Agamben. G. (1993). *Infancy and history: Essays on the destruction of experience*. London: Verso.

Ahmed, S. (1998). *Differences that matter: Feminist theory and postmodernism*. Cambridge: Cambridge University Press.

Apple, M. (1980). *Ideology and curriculum*. Boston: Routledge.

Apple, M. (1982). *Education and power*. Boston: Routledge.

Apple, M. (1988). *Teachers and texts: A political economy of class and gender relations in education*. New York: Routledge.

Questions of You

Apple, M. (1994). Series editor's introduction. In A. Gitlin (Ed.), *Power and method: Political activism and educational research* (pp. ix–xii). New York: Routledge.

Aronowitz, S., & Giroux, H. (1991). *Postmodern education: Politics, culture, and social criticism*. Minneapolis: University of Minnesota Press.

Ashton-Warner, S. (1963). *Teacher*. New York: Signet.

Barthes, R. (1975). *The pleasure of the text*. (R. Miller, Trans.). New York: Hill and Wang.

Barthes, R. (1990). The death of the author. (S. Heath, Trans.). In *Image, music, text* (pp. 142–148). New York: Hill and Wang.

Bateson, M.C. (1990). *Composing a life*. New York: Atlantic Monthly Press.

Becker, C. (Ed.). (1994). *The subversive imagination: Artists, society, and social responsibility*. New York: Routledge.

Belenky, M.F., Clinchy, B.M., Goldberger, N.R., & Tarule, J.M. (1986). *Women's ways of knowing: The development of self, voice, and mind*. New York: Basic Books.

Berg, L. (1977). *Reading and loving*. London: Routledge.

Beyer, L., & Bloch, M. (1996). Theory: An analysis (part 1). *Advances in Early Education and Day Care 8*, 21–39.

Bloom, L., & Munro, P. (1993, March). *Conflicts of selves: Interpretation and women's personal narratives*. Paper presented at the annual meeting of the American Educational Research Association, Atlanta, GA.

Britzman, D. (1994, April). *On refusing explication: A non–narrative narrativity*. Paper presented at the annual meeting of the American Educational Research Association, New Orleans, LA.

Britzman, D. (1995). Beyond innocent readings: Educational ethnography as a crisis of representation. In W. Pink & G. Noblit (Eds.), *Continuity and contradiction: The future of the sociology of education* (pp. 133–156). Cresskill, NJ: Hampton Press, Inc.

Brooks, P. (1976). *The melodramatic imagination*. New Haven: Yale University Press.

Brunner, D. (1990, February). *Creating the reflective practitioner: A role for imaginative literature in teacher education*. Paper presented at the annual meeting of the American Association of Colleges for Teacher Education. Chicago, IL.

Buford, B. (1996, June 24 & July 1). The seduction of storytelling: Why is narrative suddenly so popular? *The New Yorker*, 11–12.

Butler, J. (1990). *Gender trouble: Feminism and the subversion of identity*. New York: Routledge.

Byrne, D. (1995). *Strange ritual*. San Francisco: Chronicle Books.

Carter, F. (1986). *The education of little tree*. Albuquerque, NM: University of New Mexico Press.

Casey, K. (1993). *I answer with my life: Life histories of women teachers working for social change*. New York: Routledge.

Cisneros, S. (1985). *The house on mango street*. Houston: ArtePublico Press.

Cixous, H. (1993). *Three steps on the ladder of writing*. New York: Columbia.

Clandinin, J., & Connelly, M. (1996). Teachers' professional knowledge landscapes: Teacher stories— stories of teachers— school stories— stories of schools. *Educational Researcher 25* (3), 24–30.

Coles, R. (1989). *The call of stories: Teaching and the moral imagination*. New York: Pantheon.

Council on Interracial Books for Children. (1976). *Human values in children's books*. New York: Council on Interracial Books for Children.

Deleuze, G., & Guattari, F. (1987). *A Thousand Plateaus*. (B. Massumi, Trans.) Minneapolis: University of Minnesota Press.

Delpit, L. (1988). The silenced dialogue: Power and pedagogy in educating other people's children. *Harvard Educational Review 58* (3), 280–297.

Denzin, N. (1995). The poststructuralist crisis in the social sciences: Learning from James Joyce. In R. H. Brown (Ed.), *Postmodern representations: Truth, power, and memisis in the human sciences* (pp. 38–59). Urbana: University of Illinois Press.

Dewey, J. (1952). *Art as experience*. New York: Capricorn. (Original work published in 1934)

Diamond, C. T. P., & Mullen, C. (Eds.). (1999). *The Postmodern educator: Arts-based inquiries and teacher development.* New York: Peter Lang.

Dixon, R. (1977). *Catching them while they are young. Volume 1: Sex, race, and class in children's books.* London: Pluto Press.

Donmoyer, R. (1991). The first glamourizer of thought: Theoretical and autobiographical ruminations on drama and education. In G. Willis & W. Schubert (Eds.), *Reflections from the heart of educational inquiry: Understanding curriculum and teaching through the arts* (pp. 90–106). Albany, NY: SUNY-Albany Press.

Donmoyer, R. (1996). Educational research in an era of paradigm proliferation: What's a journal editor to do? *Educational Researcher 25* (2), 19–25.

Dostoyevsky, F. (1979). *The grand inquisitor on the nature of man.* Indianapolis, IN: Bobbs-Merrill.

DuPlessis, R. (1990). *The pink guitar: Writing as feminist practice.* New York: Routledge.

Egan, K. (1986). *Teaching as storytelling.* London, Ontario, Canada: Althouse Press.

Egan, K. (1988). *Imagination and education.* New York: Teachers College Press.

Eisner, E. (1997). The promise and perils of alternative forms of data representation. *Educational Researcher 26* (6), 4–10.

Ellman, L. (1998). *Man or mango?* New York: Farrar, Straus & Giroux.

Eliot, G. (1988). *Middlemarch: A study of provincial life.* New York: Knopf.

Emecheta, B. (1979). *The joys of motherhood.* New York: G. Braziller.

Felman, S., & Laub, M. (1992). *Testimony: Crises of witnessing in literature, psychoanalysis, and history.* New York: Routledge.

Fetterley, J. (1978). *The resisting reader: A feminist approach to American fiction.* Bloomington, IN: Indiana University Press.

Foucault, M. (1988). *Politics, philosophy, culture: Interviews and other writings (1977-1984).* (L. Kritzman, Trans.). New York: Routledge.

Freire, P. (1998). *Teachers as cultural workers.* Boulder, CO: Westview.

Gilmore, L. (1994). *Autobiographics: A feminist theory of women's self-representation.* Ithaca, NY: Cornell University Press.

Giroux, H., Lankshear, C., McLaren, P. & Peters, M. (1996). *Counternarratives: Cultural studies and critical pedagogies in postmodern spaces.* New York: Routledge.

Gomez-Pena, G. (1994). The free art agreement/El tratado de libre culture. In C. Becker (Ed.), *The subversive imagination: Artists, society, and social responsibility* (pp. 208-222). New York: Routledge.

Greene, M. (1973). *Teacher as stranger: Educational philosophy for the modern age.* Belmont, CA: Wadsworth.

Greene, M. (1978). *Landscapes of learning.* New York: Teachers College Press.

Greene, M. (1994). Postmodernism and the crisis of representation. *English Education 26* (4), 206–219.

Griffin, S. (1982). Voices. In *Made from this earth: An anthology of writings.* (pp. 278–323). New York: Harper and Row.

Grumet, M. (1988). *Bitter milk: Women and teaching.* Amherst, MA: University of Massachusetts Press.

Grumet, M. (1991). The politics of personal knowledge. In C. Witherell & N. Noddings (Eds.), *Stories lives tell: Narrative and dialogue in education* (pp. 67–77). New York Teachers College Press.

Hall, E. (1984). *The dance of life: Other dimensions of time.* New York: Anchor.

Hamilton, V. (1971). *The planet of Junior Brown.* New York. Dell.

Harding, S. (1987). *Feminism and methodology.* London: Routledge.

Hauser, M. (1998). In our own backyards: Whose view? In M. Hauser & J. Jipson (Eds.), *Intersections: Feminisms and early childhoods* (pp. 137–145). New York: Peter Lang.

hooks, b. (1994). *Teaching to transgress: Education as the practice of freedom.* New York: Routledge.

James, H. (1992). The real thing. In *The Portable Henry James.* New York: Penguin. (Original work published in 1892)

Jipson, J., Munro, P., Victor, S., Froude Jones, K, & Freed–Rowland, B. (1995). *Repositioning feminism and education: Perspectives on educating for social change.* Westport, CT: Bergin & Garvey.

Jipson, J., & Paley, N. (1991). The selective tradition in teachers' choice of children's literature: Does it exist in the elementary classroom? *English Education 23* (3), 148–159.

Jipson, J., & Paley, N. (1992a). Is there a base to today's literature-based reading programs? *English Education 24* (2), 77–90.

Jipson, J., & Paley, N. (1992b). Fiction as curricular text. *Educational Foundations 6* (2), 21–33.

Jipson, J., & Paley, N. (1994). Literature/curriculum/authority/absence: A parallel conversation. *English Education 26* (4), 220–235.

Jipson, J., & Paley, N. (Eds.). (1997). *Daredevil research: Re-creating analytic practice.* New York: Peter Lang.

Jipson, J., & Paley, N. (1999). Animals and curriculum masters. In C. T. P. Diamond & C. Mullen (Eds.), *The postmodern educator: Arts–based inquiries and teacher development* (pp. 409–422). New York: Peter Lang.

Kingsolver, B. (1988). *The bean trees.* New York: Harper and Row.

Kozol, J. (1988). *Rachel and her children.* New York: Crown.

Lather, P. (1991). *Getting smart: Feminist research and pedagogy with/in the postmodern.* New York: Routledge.

Lather, P. (1999, October). *Reading the image of Rigoberta Menchu: Undecidability and language lessons.* Paper presented at the Conference of Curriculum Theory and Classroom Practice, Dayton, OH.

Levin, D. (1993). *Modernity and the hegemony of vision.* Berkeley, CA: University of California Press.

Lessing, D. (1988). *The fifth child.* New York: Knopf.

Luke, A., Cooke, J., & Luke, C. (1986). The selective tradition in action: Gender bias in student teachers' selections of children's literature. *English Education 18* (4), 209–218.

Marcuse, H. (1964). *One dimensional man.* Boston: Beacon Press.

Miller, J. (1990). *Creating spaces and finding voices: Teachers collaborating for empowerment.* Albany, NY: State University of New York Press

Miller, N. (1991). *Getting personal: Feminist occasions and other autobiographical acts.* New York: Routledge.

Moore, M. (1980). *Man of the high country.* New York: Harlequin.

Morrison, T. (1987). *Beloved.* New York: Knopf.

Mullen, C., Cox, M.D., Boetcher, C.K., & Adoue, D.S. (Eds.). (1997). *Breaking the circle of one: Redefining mentorship in the lives and writings of educators.* New York: Peter Lang.

Page, H. (1988). Literature across the college curriculum. *The Journal of Reading 31*, 520–523.

Paley, N. (1988). Kids of survival: Experiments in the study of literature. *English Journal 77* (5), 54–58.

Paley, N. (1995). *Finding art's place: Experiments in contemporary education and culture.* New York: Routledge.

Paley, N., & Jipson, J. (1995, April). *Research, repetition, anti–memory: A reexamination of the selective tradition in teachers' choice of children's literature.* An electronic research performance presented at the annual meeting of the American Educational Research Association, San Francisco, CA.

Paley, N., & Jipson, J. (1997a). Duplications. *Taboo: The Journal of Culture and Education 2* (2), 269.

Paley, N., & Jipson, J. (1997b). Personal history: Researching literature and curriculum (literal, alter, hyper). *English Education 29* (1), 59–69.

Perry, A. (1993). *Rutland place.* New York: Fawcett Crest.

Pinar, W. (1988). Whole, bright, deep with understanding: Issues in qualitative research and autobiographical method. In W. Pinar (Ed.), *Contemporary curriculum discourses* (pp. 134–153). Scottsdale, AZ: Gorsuch Scarisbrick.

Read, H. (1943). *Education through art.* London: Faber and Faber.

Shannon, P. (1986). Hidden within the pages: A study of social perspective in young children's favorite books. *The Reading Teacher 39* (7), 656–663.

Slapin, B., & Seale, D. (Eds.). (1988). *Books without bias: Through Indian eyes.* Berkeley, CA: Oyate.

Smith, S. (1993). *Subjectivity, identity, and the body: Women's autobiographical practices in the twentieth century*. Bloomington, IN: Indiana University Press.

Soto, G. (1990). *A fire in my hands*. New York: Scholastic.

Stainton-Rogers, R., & W. (1992). *Stories of childhood: Shifting agendas of child concern*. Toronto: University of Toronto.

Steiner, G. (1989). *Real presences*. Chicago: University of Chicago Press.

Taxel, J. (1981). The outsiders of the American revolution: The selective tradition in children's fiction. *Interchange 12* (2–3), 206–228.

Taxel, J. (1983). The American revolution in children's fiction. *Research in the Teaching of English 17* (1), 61–83.

Taylor, M., & Saarinen, E. (1995). *Imagologies: Media philosophy*. New York: Routledge.

Trinh, M. (1991). *When the moon waxes red: Representation, gender, and cultural politics*. New York: Routledge.

Trinh, M. (1992). *Framer framed*. New York: Routledge.

Wald, A. (1981). Hegemony and literary tradition in America. *Humanities in Society 4*, 419–430.

Welch, J. (1986). *Fools crow*. New York: Viking.

Williams, (1977). *Marxism and literature*. Oxford: Oxford University Press.

Willis, G., & Schubert, W. (Eds.). (1991). *Reflections from the heart of educational inquiry: Understanding curriculum and teaching through the arts*. Albany, NY: SUNY–Albany Press.

Wolcott, H. (1990). On seeking— and rejecting— validity in qualitative research. In E. Eisner & A. Peshkin (Eds.), *Qualitative inquiry in education* (pp. 121–152). New York: Teachers College Press.

Wolcott. H. (1994). *Transforming qualitative data*. Newbury Park, CA: Sage.

Woolf, V. (1938). *Three guineas*. New York: Harcourt, Brace and Company.

Zinn, H. (1980). *The 20th century: A people's history*. New York: Harper and Row.

A
and

Always looking for you

attachment (non-)
avarice[1]
astonished

atonement
anarchy   semi-double
                                                 Always separate or just

---

This chapter experiments with ritual external processes of listing and directing readers to subjects referred to within the text. It was designed to evoke subjective processes floating in the spaces between such ordered realities.

The format of this section is intentional.

another
anger/affection

again all (gone)

(that needs to be kept

Alive)

allege
a ledge

all edge

B
bother

But this in some ways also

brother (ly)
bargained-for[2]   sets us free.
bay
Banyan tree
brood[3]
boundaries
borders
be

C
compliant   Can try to name it.
complicit   Can try to know it.
complacent   Can try to see it.
CA (the state)   Can try to show it.
champagne (see CA)   Can try to feel it.

calibrate

(Chance and definity:

how far can this
schizophrenia be

celebrate
concern
cinzano
Caliban

pushed?)

correct
corrupt
core
certainty
conscientious (sp.)

D
determine
Dare Devil (Research)
daredevil
delicious

Double (bind?)

delirious
dream
dawn
dessert
desert
delicate
deny

delight
decent (in-)
descent[4]
dare
devil
double
delete

E
eternity

                                        Expectations: those which
                                        place

eloquence

                                        obligations on us to be so
                                        sure (how
empiricism   will we ever find the ones
                                        we've lost?)

eccentricism
Erik & Emily[5]
emotion
elation
emission
emerge
essence
entirety (in its)
erehwon[6]

edge

F
fish

friend

feeling
fragments?

Faithful to this even
though maybe
faith is not enough.

G
glen (Flora)
glory
grateful
gratuitous (See Lethal Weapon IV)

grandma
granite
Granita
generate
getting
gone (all-)

H
help
high (light)   Hunger.

heaven

horrific

halo

here-to-for
hegemony[7]

hope

I
ice

intense
imagination(s)
imitate
ingrate

imposition

idea   Inquiring, not defining

ideal
ideation
idle (idol)
index
inter-subjectivity
I

J
joint
jump

join
justice
Jenny[8]
jagged (edge?) (little pill?)
justice (again)

K
keep

kin

ken

know

L
Leisure

                    Like you've just come
                    home to a place

loss

                    you've never been
                    because it never was.

limp   (lack of what?)

lone   (lone for whom?)

limit

lucid

M
mountain
manifold

Mentor/tormentor

manipulate

manatee   My/you?

mandate

manly

map[9]

N
notice
nick (N)
nice
neat

norm
nature
native
nascent

O
oasis[10]

Once there was a way to
get back homeward;

once we knew a
way
to get back home.

One day, they found it
dead in its
cage

Or hope.

qualms
quotient
quarrel
quintessential
quality
querulous
quandary
questions
query
quarry
quaint
queasy

R
rage
rendezvous
reservation
reticent
reluctance

                                        Run, run run, run,

Runaway.
re(verberate)
re(enact)
re(position)
re(present)

S
safe
sensuous
solitary

sacred   Silence that can no longer
                                          be performed

silent

sacrifice
sole
suppose
sense
silence[11]

T
torrent
                                          Two some

turbulence
time
teach
torrid

                                          These strange searchings
                                          and companion
                                          desires,

terrible

                                          Twins sometimes,
trenchant[12]   Then others,
                                          why

tedious
trouble

U
unctuous

V
vary
victim
vantage
voice
vortex
verse
version

vestments (-in)
venerable
vengeance
vendor
vicissitudes
voice(s)

W
wait

why
wholesome
worry
will

We began slowly, not
knowing, not really sure
about what might

                    happen
or what was right.

Would this help us escape
some of the old Stories
and how they tend to
conclude in the one
remember?

X
x-cited
x-clamation
x-pendable

Y   You were uncertain about
                                 this?

you

Z
zealot
zap
zone

NOTES

[1] I just like the sound of this word.

[2] As in "not what they had."

[3] In both senses of the word.

[4] See also Lessing, D. (19xx). *Briefing for a descent into hell.*

[5] Jan's kids.

[6] Everywhere.

[7] And related h words: Habermas, hermeneutics, helio(trope).

[8] Jan's other daughter.

[9] Also Mixx, Milton, Madison, Monterey, and montage.

[10] Where did that oasis we made for each other go?

[11] One of the essentials.

[12] I like the sound of this word, too.

Studies in the Postmodern Theory of Education

General Editors
Joe L. Kincheloe & Shirley R. Steinberg

Counterpoints publishes the most compelling and imaginative books being written in education today. Grounded on the theoretical advances in criticalism, feminism, and postmodernism in the last two decades of the twentieth century, Counterpoints engages the meaning of these innovations in various forms of educational expression. Committed to the proposition that theoretical literature should be accessible to a variety of audiences, the series insists that its authors avoid esoteric and jargonistic languages that transform educational scholarship into an elite discourse for the initiated. Scholarly work matters only to the degree it affects consciousness and practice at multiple sites. Counterpoints' editorial policy is based on these principles and the ability of scholars to break new ground, to open new conversations, to go where educators have never gone before.

For additional information about this series or for the submission of manuscripts, please contact:

Joe L. Kincheloe & Shirley R. Steinberg
637 West Foster Avenue
State College, PA 16801

To order other books in this series, please contact our Customer Service Department at:

(800) 770-LANG (within the U.S.)
(212) 647-7706 (outside the U.S.)
(212) 647-7707 FAX

or browse online by series at:
www.peterlang.com